Contents

Acknowledgements

The papers by John Villiers and Professor K. Mathew were originally presented at the second International Conference on Indian Ocean Studies (ICIOS II) which was held in Perth, Western Australia, in December 1984. They were presented at the session on the history of the Portuguese in the Indian Ocean Region which was chaired by Dr M. N. Pearson. The editor would like to thank Colin Jones, Robert Massey and Michael Duffy for help with the proof reading and Seán Goddard who designed the cover.

PORTUGUESE COLONIAL EMPIRE

edited by Malyn Newitt

EXETER STUDIES IN HISTORY No.11

Published by the University of Exeter 1986

EXETER STUDIES IN HISTORY

General Editor

C.D.H.Jones BA DPhil FRHistS

Editorial Committee

Printed in Great Britain by A. Wheaton & Co. Ltd., Exeter

ISBN 0 85989 257 3

ISSN 0260 8626

Introduction

MALYN NEWITT

It is usual today to think of Portugal as having had three distinct phases in her imperial history. The "first empire" was founded in 1415, developing as a maritime, commercial enterprise in Africa and Asia. The "second empire" was an Atlantic one based on slaves, sugar and gold in which Angola and Brazil were the major partners. It lasted until Brazil became independent in 1825. The "third empire" was that founded in Africa at the time of the "scramble", which survived until the Portuguese Revolution of 1974. This collection of essays deals with the first phase of Portuguese imperial history.

The English-speaking student approaching the topic of Iberian expansion finds an astonishing contrast in the quality and quantity of the literature available. The overseas empire of Spain in the sixteenth century is the subject of a vast literature in English and interest in, and debate about it, has been considerable from the time of Queen Elizabeth to the present. Information about the Portuguese empire is much more sketchy. There are few good biographies of the leading personalities and even fewer good outlines of the development of the empire. In part this is due to the fact that the Portuguese possessions were widely scattered throughout the world with each of its regions becoming a separate field of activity. A coherent narrative of the development of the empire, therefore, becomes nearly impossible and has defeated all those who have tried to produce one. Instead a number of detailed monographs exist, reflecting the specialist area of interest of the writers. The areas best served by these monographs are China, Japan, East and West Africa and Brazil. In general the seventeenth century, the century of decline, is better covered than the sixteenth, the century of growth. Huge gaps exist in the literature. Southeast Asia is very poorly covered, and the history of the Persian Gulf and Sri Lanka in the sixteenth century is a virtual blank. However, the biggest gap of all is India. Although two of the writers

represented in this book, K.S.Mathew and A.R.Disney, together with
M.N.Pearson have produced a series of valuable monographs on the
economic and commercial history of Portuguese India, no general
study of the Portuguese in eastern and western India has appeared
since Danvers and Whiteway wrote at the end of the last century,
and anyone familiar with their writings will appreciate their very
great limitations. It might be thought that the fifteenth
century, where at least the voyages of discovery form a coherent
narrative theme, would be better covered and there are, in fact,
numerous publications purporting to deal with the discovery of the
sea route to India. However, writing in English has not reflected
the best work of the Portuguese economic historians and has
largely ignored areas of activity like North Africa. Above all
there are very few studies of Portugal itself and it is fair to
say that, for all periods of its history, but especially for the
fifteenth and sixteenth centuries, Portugal remains less
well-known than its empire.

The essays in this book focus on four of the fields that
are less well-covered in writings available to the English reader
– the economic and social history of the "Discoveries", Southeast
Asia and the Portuguese in the western India.

In most English publications the origins of the
Portuguese overseas empire are still represented as deliberate
planning on the part of the Portuguese royal family, especially
Prince Henry the Navigator (1394-1460), King João II (1481-95) and
King Manuel (1495-1521). Reaching India by sea was the conscious
objective almost from the start and the motives were, at least in
part, religious and political. To a large extent the figure of
Henry himself has been demythologised in recent writing and he is
no longer portrayed as hero, saint, scholar and scientist, but he
is still given the central role in the planning and organising of
the discoveries as though they were a personal enterprise on his
part.

In the first essay in this collection I have tried to
give a more organic and evolutionary view of the origins of the
Portuguese expansion and to present some of the ideas of the most
important of the modern Portuguese historians, Vitorino Magalhães
Godinho, which have been unjustly neglected by English writers.
According to this view Portuguese expansion grew out of the
maritime activity of the fourteenth century which had seen Genoese
planting trading factories in North Africa and the ships of
various nationalities indulging in piracy and slaving off the
Moroccan coast and in the Canary islands. The new departure in
the fifteenth century was not to sail down the African coast but
to launch major expeditions against Morocco in an attempt to take
the reconquista across the straits. The reasons behind this
decision lie in Portuguese social and economic conditions at the
end of the fourteenth century. After a period of civil war and
plague, the economy was severely dislocated with extensive rural

depopulation, food shortages, an absence of ready money and a collapse in royal revenues. Invading the rich agricultural lands of Morocco had a great appeal to all classes in Portugal and, with one significant break in the 1440s when the Infante Dom Pedro was regent, it remained the major objective of Portuguese policy in the fifteenth century. Far more resources were poured into the North African expeditions than were ever devoted to African voyaging or, indeed, to the empire in the East in the sixteenth century. Yet, apart from the capture of a few coastal towns, nothing ever came of the <u>reconquista</u> in North Africa and, as an empire, it was stillborn. Nevertheless the Moroccan wars satisfied the ambitions of the nobility who wanted to exercise commands, establish their military reputations and obtain plunder and ransoms which would enrich them in a way acceptable to current ideals of chivalry. Moreover Morocco was close at hand and involved far less risk than the enterprises in Africa and the East.

The Portuguese empire was born of piracy and slave raiding carried on by the <u>fidalgos</u> (knights) and supported by the church, the royal princes and the great nobles who needed to find employment, preferably outside Portugal, for their retainers. However, it was transformed by two factors. The first of these was the expansion of sugar growing, financed by Genoese capital, from Portugal itself to the Atlantic islands, Madeira and the Canaries, and later Cape Verde and São Tomé. Sugar, and other crops like wheat and wine, provided a sound base for the settlement of the island groups and attracted merchants and peasants, as well as the <u>fidalgo</u> class and the ever-greedy higher nobility.

The second factor was the painful discovery that slave raiding would be bloodily rebuffed by the well-armed and well-organised black kingdoms south of the Senegal river. Within a few years of making contact with black Africa the Portuguese realised that these societies were too formidable to be raided with impunity. On the other hand, trade was not only possible but positively welcomed. For the first, and probably the only, time in their imperial history the Portuguese found themselves well-placed economically to capture a local market. The black states imported fine cloths, horses, wheat and salt. These had previously been brought expensively across the Sahara from North Africa; now the Portuguese could bring them more cheaply and directly by sea. Moreover Portugal herself was a producer of all these commodities. Horses were bred in the peninsula or Morocco, wheat came from Madeira, salt from Aveiro and later from the massive deposits in the Cape Verde archipelago and cloth could be obtained from Morocco or was produced for the African market in the Cape Verde islands. All these commodities could be traded profitably in the African market and, not surprisingly, the merchant houses of Venice and Genoa hastened to establish their position in this commerce, particularly when the gold of West

Africa began to be siphoned away from North African markets towards the trading posts (or "factories") established under Portuguese auspices on the coast.

The fifteen century saw certain trends emerge which were to characterise the empire in its maturity in the sixteenth century. First were the crown monopolies. In the fifteenth century a monopoly of all trade with Guinea was granted to Prince Henry which, on his death, was transferred to the crown. Within the overall concept of a crown monopoly various concessions were made. Sometimes the trade as a whole, or parts of it, would be leased to individuals or syndicates. The trade of Arguim, for example, was leased by Henry to a syndicate, while in 1469 Fernão Gomes, a Lisbon merchant, obtained the lease of the whole Guinea trade. Another expedient was for the trade in certain commodities to be leased and such agreements were made with the donatory "captains" of the islands. Just occasionally the crown tried the direct exploitation of the trade itself. The most notable example of this was the gold trade of Mina where a fort was established in 1482 in which a royal factor carried on trade on the crown's behalf.

The second trend to emerge in the fifteenth century was the pattern of participation by the fidalgo class. The Portuguese nobility were at first interested in overseas expansion in order to obtain offices and to enrich themselves with the spoils of war. They were also interested in acquiring the quasi-feudal grants of donatory captaincies in the islands, in Brazil and Angola which allowed them to exercise a wide-ranging political authority while enjoying lucrative economic privileges. The establishment of the empire in the East opened up a vast new range of opportunities. However, if the nobility were primarily a political and military elite, they were increasingly prepared to dabble in commerce inspite of the currently prevailing idea that commerce involved a derogation of status. What allowed them to make the transition from office-holding to commerce was the habit of the crown of leasing its monopolies. If a noble acquired the right to exercise the crown's trade monopoly, he was acquiring the right to exercise part of the royal prerogative. Moreover, he was able in his turn to sublease the trading rights so that he did not have to take part in commerce directly himself. In this way trade became an aspect of the holding of office and the wielding of political power. By the middle of the sixteenth century the leasing of the royal monopolies, either to the fortress captains or in the form of viagens dos lugares (monopoly voyages), had become the dominant mode of operation within the empire.

A third tendency, already clearly present in the fifteenth century, was for the empire to become self-supporting and to generate its own dynamic for further expansion, independent of Portugal itself. By the middle of the fifteenth century commercial expansion in West Africa was already being undertaken

partly by settlers from the Atlantic islands and was increasingly
dependent on the development of various "local" trades, rather
than on direct trade with Portugal. The settlers of Madeira took
their wheat to West Africa and returned with slaves for the sugar
plantations. The profits of sugar were used to open up new
plantations in the island groups like the Cape Verde and Guinea
islands. The Cape Verdians traded their salt and cotton cloth in
Upper Guinea and rapidly established a creole trading community
there. Later the gold trade of Mina came to depend on the
Portuguese developing a "local" trade in bark cloth, cowrie shells
and slaves from the Congo region. The thriving commercial empire
in West Africa was run by a creole community which was born and
bred in Africa and which had only the most tenuous links with
Portugal. The same tendency immediately manifested itself in the
East where the Portuguese found that they had to become involved
in the "country" trade if they were to compete at all in Asiatic
markets.

The system which had developed to handle the trade of
West Africa matured once the Portuguese established themselves in
the East. John Villiers' article shows in detail how the empire
evolved in the huge arena of Southeast Asia. He points out that
it had little formal structure. The Portuguese controlled
virtually no territory and there was no legal framework for the
various communities and enterprises that were loosely entitled the
Estado da India. The formal part of the empire consisted of a
series of trading factories (feitorias) and forts (fortalezas).
The latter were few and far between, the former rather more
common. They acted as centres from which the royal monopoly in
certain commodities like cloves, silk, sandalwood etc. would be
operated but they were also centres of a much wider and more
shadowy informal empire. This was made up of Portuguese traders
who were scattered throughout the islands, founding their own
commercial communities, intermarrying with the local populations
and establishing their own political relations with the islands'
rulers. The largest of these independent merchant communities was
the one established at Macao. This was eventually partially
incorporated into the Estado da India by being granted the right
to establish a town council (Senado da Câmara) but it never had a
captain or governor and there was never a royal fort there, nor
did the Chinese cede sovereignty over Macao to the Portuguese.

The church also contributed to the informal nature of the
Portuguese empire. Most missionary activity by the Franciscans,
Augustinians and Jesuits took place in areas where there was no
Portuguese jurisdiction. The successful missions came to be
nucleii of native and half-caste christian populations which were
loosely associated with the Estado da India through the padroado
real, the crown's right of patronage which allowed it to have
jurisdiction over all mission and church establishments in the
East.

As John Villiers points out, the Estado da India, because it had no real legal format, is a very elusive empire to describe or to comprehend. In Southeast Asia it assumed varied levels of informality from the great captaincy of Malacca with its fort, garrison and town council, and the great quasi-independent commercial centres of Macao and Jesuit-dominated Nagasaki, to the half-caste trading communities and isolated missions scattered throughout the Islands. These tiny communities of half-caste or native christians were entirely local in the focus of their activities and had little or no contact with any centres of Portuguese power, let alone with Lisbon. Most of the trade they conducted was local in character and in many parts of the East the "Portuguese" simply became a trading caste alongside other castes and ethnic communities.

Nevertheless, there were always threads, however slender, which bound the parts of the empire to the centre. As already mentioned, there was the padroado real and the jurisdiction which this allowed the Portuguese king to claim to wield even over the christian subjects of other monarchs. There was also the royal license to undertake monopoly voyages (viagens dos lugares). According to this system the Portuguese crown would sell the right to operate a trading ship on a given route, usually for a single round voyage. The buyer of the "voyage", who often had the backing of a merchant syndicate, would then freight the ship in part himself and lease space in it to other merchants. The profits to be made from these voyages could be immense when they carried with them the right to exercise the royal monopoly in certain products. However, many of the voyages that were sold, particularly in Southeast Asia, were in areas where the Portuguese had never even claimed to have a trading monopoly. In this case the profits were derived from the quasi-political status of the purchaser. This can be seen most clearly in the case of the famous voyage from Goa to Macao and Nagasaki, the captain of which was also governor of the Portuguese in China and Japan for the season.

The crown's custom of selling profitable trade monopolies to captains of fortresses for a single voyage or for three years enabled huge personal fortunes to be amassed in "one-off" enterprises but certainly inhibited the growth of capitalism as none of the syndicates assembled to finance the voyages had the resources or were able to envisage the long term investments of the Dutch and English chartered companies.

All these monopolies ultimately derived from the monopolies that the Portuguese crown claimed over certain commodities in eastern trade. Soon after the formal establishment of their power in the western Indian Ocean, the crown had claimed the exclusive right to trade in pepper, gold, ivory, horses, cinnamon and cloves. Later other commodities would be added to the list. The Portuguese also claimed the right to license all

Asiatic shipping, to force it to pay customs dues at Portuguese ports and to issue it with a cartaz or safeconduct. Professor Mathew shows how the system of cartazes was operated in the western Indian Ocean, the region which could be dominated by the Portuguese forts at Mozambique, Ormuz, Diu, Goa and Colombo.

Initially the cartaz was issued as a safeconduct during the struggle for naval supremacy in the Indian Ocean. It then became a means for securing the royal monopoly in certain commodities, as a cartaz was only issued on condition that the vessel was not carrying any of the forbidden merchandise. Later the cartaz became little more than a device for taxing Asiatic shipping and obtaining revenue for the Portuguese crown. The Portuguese kings claimed that, in the same way that other sovereigns ruled areas of land, taxed merchants and levied customs duties at the ports of entry, they ruled the sea and also had the right to levy taxes on merchants who crossed their domain.

That this right to rule the seas had no precedent in Asia or Asiatic law goes almost without saying. It had very little foundation in European law either and was precariously based on papal grants which the Portuguese crown chose to believe had some universal applicability. In reality the system depended on force. However, as Professor Mathew points out, force is not the sole explanation because the Portuguese were never able to control the seas to anything like the extent needed to impose their will on Asiatic shipping and could not prevent trade in forbidden commodities from being sent overland. Moreover, Asian shipowners continued to obtain cartazes from the Portuguese even when their power was being everywhere challenged by the far more formidable Dutch. The cartaz was cheap and only oppressive as a tax in that it forced ships to call at Portuguese ports to pay dues. Many ship owners came to pay it as a matter of course, as one form of insurance, before embarking on a trading voyage.

Initially the Estado da India was a maritime and commercial enterprise and the king of Portugal possessed only a few fortified ports as bases for his fleet. However, as the sixteenth century wore on, the Portuguese came to acquire more and mnore territory and to rule directly African and Asian populations numbering in millions. The areas of Portuguese territorial control were in the Zambesi valley (and in the Cuanza valley in Angola), in Sri Lanka, in northern India and in the neighbourhood of Goa. Portuguese rule in India, as opposed to their commercial, religious and foreign political relations, is a topic neglected by English-speaking historians and Anthony Disney's article is of crucial importance in focussing on the web of private trading ventures, territorial interests and fixed assets that Goa represented in the seventeenth century. After 1640, as a result of the struggle with the Dutch, the city ceased to be the military and administrative centre of a vast empire. Instead it became a small Indian state. While the formal structure of the empire crumbled away, trade with Europe shrank, and Goa itself was subject to Dutch blockade and harrassment, private trade continued to flourish with the viceroys and officials leading the way in making huge personal fortunes while the royal treasury was empty and the defences of the city stripped bare.

The decay of Goa's commercial and political importance was gradual. One of the factors that delayed the decline was the increasing power and prestige of the religious orders all of whom had their headquarters in the "Rome of the Orient". The vast wealth of the church was reflected in the impressive ecclesiastical architecture of the seventeenth century, the great mannerist cathedrals and conventual churches rising as the commercial suburbs of the city became deserted and the population declined. Eventually the city of Goa disappeared altogether and the great churches were left stranded amid the encroaching jungle. Disney points out that the decline of Goa was not just the result of the decline of Portuguese power. The city had too small a hinterland and could never feed itself adequately. Moreover the demographic decline, which was made irreversible by the great famine of 1630-1, was an independent factor helping to create the crisis for the city.

The first Portuguese empire survived in a twilight that never quite darkened into total night. While the "second empire", built on sugar, gold and slaves, enjoyed its heyday in the seventeenth and eighteenth centuries, the last relics of the eastern empire lingered on. The ivory trade kept alive the settlements in eastern Africa; Indian traders from Diu enjoyed a continuing prosperity and in the remote Far East Macao and Timor remained outposts of the old empire. John Villiers depicts the nature of the regime that survived in Timor in the eighteenth and early nineteenth centuries. It was reminiscent of the equally exotic Portuguese survival in the Zambesi valley. Power lay entirely with the local "Portuguese" community - powerful clans with Portuguese names and a vestigial catholic faith but much intermarried with the local peoples and culturally indistinguishable from them. Portuguese governors held office on sufferance and made little attempt to enforce any kind of law or administration in the interior. The reality of Portuguese Timor was the sandalwood trade which remained important and profitable, and the families who controlled this trade were the real rulers of the land. The importance of such survivals was that, as in eastern Africa, they could be made the basis for claims to territory when the scramble for empire once more became feverish in the nineteenth century. Indeed the whole of Portugal's "third empire" was built on the vestigial survivals of her first.

Prince Henry and the Origins of Portuguese Expansion

MALYN NEWITT

Introduction

It may seem superfluous to write yet another article about the origins of the Portuguese overseas empire. This is one of the most frequently discussed historical topics and, after so much controversy, it might seem that there is nothing new that can possibly be said about it. Yet although scarcely a year passes without some publication in English dealing with this subject, many of the most important ideas relating to it are either inaccessibly hidden away in minor publications or have never been made comprehensibly available in English. The object of this article, therefore, is to look at some of the issues that have preoccupied historians of this period but which have not been fully discussed in English publications.

'Tramping in its own footsteps, without ever leaving the closed circle, the ox tirelessly turns the waterwheel ... so with the history of the discoveries, the same problems posed and reposed, the same theses indefatigably re-examined from the same point of view'.(1) In this way Vitorino Magalhães Godinho started his survey of the literature of the discoveries. He was referring to the seemingly endless publications of the school of historians which has concerned itself almost exclusively with the "facts" of the period. These historians have painstakingly sought to establish the chronology of the voyages and have often seemed to confine the study of their history to answering the apparently fascinating question, 'who discovered what first?'. The intriguing nature of the detective work clearly lies in the fact that the record of early European expansion is very meagre indeed and clues are often tantalisingly inconclusive. Nevertheless over the years the work of this school has led to basic agreement on the chronology of Portuguese expansion and it seems sensible to begin by summarising this as it is more or less the only point of real agreement among opposing factions of historians.

The Aviz dynasty acquired the Portuguese throne in 1385 with English help. In 1415 a successful attack was made on the Moroccan port of Ceuta which was garrisoned thereafter by the Portuguese. Portuguese settlement of Madeira began in 1424 and in the same year an attempt was made to conquer the Canary Islands. The Azores group of islands was regularly visited from 1427 and its settlement began in the 1430s. In 1437 an unsuccessful attack was launched against Tangier which left one of the royal princes a prisoner in Moroccan hands. In 1434 Portuguese ships sailed south of Cape Bojador and between 1441 and 1448 the whole African coast as far south as the modern Guinea-Bissau was visited and explored. From 1443 regular stops were made at Arguim island on the Mauretanian coast and by 1455 a permanent factory existed there. In 1449 the former regent, Dom Pedro, was defeated and killed at the battle of Alfarrobeira and the Braganza faction came to dominate the court of the young Afonso V. Between 1452 and 1456 Portugal secured papal bulls granting her sovereignty on the African coast and in 1458 a successful attack was launched against the Moroccan town of Alcacer. Prince Henry died in 1460. During the 1450s it does not appear that the Portuguese explored any further down the coast of Africa but the Cape Verde Islands were discovered and their settlement was begun in 1462, while in 1461 a trading voyage appears to have got as far as the coast of Sierre Leone. Thereafter no further progress was recorded until 1469 when the Lisbon merchant, Fernão Gomes, leased the Guinea trade and in the space of five years opened up the African coast as far as the modern Cameroons.

Although there is some argument about the minutiae of this chronology and about the exact role of certain individual navigators, this general outline of the period is widely accepted and is meticulously set out in Bailey Diffie's chapters in Foundations of the Portuguese Empire, published in 1977. There is, however, less agreement about the causes and the exact significance of these events. The problem arises partly from the fact that the Portuguese "discoveries" have always been seen as the beginning of the modern expansion of Europe overseas with all that that has entailed for the development of the modern world. Not surprisingly, ideological knives have been sharpened over developments so decisive in the mainstream of world history. However, disagreement arises also from the nature of the sources which record the origins of Portuguese expansion.

Of the royal chroniclers who recorded Portuguese history up to 1450, Fernão Lopes and Gomes Eannes de Azurara were contemporaries of the events they described and had access to royal archives and other documents. As medieval chroniclers go, they were remarkably well-informed and wrote either at first hand or after direct communication with the participants. Azurara deliberately set out to give a complete account of the exploits in Morocco and, in the Chronicle of the Discovery and Conquest of Guinea (hereafter Chronicle), to give a full description of the exploration of the West African coast. Azurara's chronicles can be supplemented by the accounts of Diogo Gomes and Alvise da Cadamosto, who themselves sailed to Guinea but who wrote some time after the events they described, and by the writings of the historians of the next generation, notably Duarte Pacheco Pereira and João de Barros. They can also be supplemented by numerous charters, letters and commercial documents that bear on the discoveries, by maps and the writings of non-Portuguese who knew something of the events. Nevertheless Azurara's chronicles are of overriding importance, such that if one were to take them away it would prove next to impossible to give any coherent account of the period at all. Yet historians need to be very wary as they approach Azurara's writings. The richness of the detail and the coherence of the narrative have almost always proved irresistibly seductive, but it has been the allurement of the Sirens and historians who follow Azurara too closely find their history transformed into the image that the chronicler planned for them five centuries ago.

Many historians have been aware of the problems posed by Azurara's chronicles, and none more so than P. E. Russell who, with an interval of 23 years between them, wrote two important articles on Prince Henry and his chronicler - neither of them, unfortunately, very accessible for the general reader. The problems may be summarised as follows. First, Azurara completed his Chronicle sometime in the early 1450s, probably 1453, and tells the story of the "discoveries" up to 1448. He wrote in the immediate aftermath of the short civil war that led to the death of the Infante Dom Pedro in 1449 and the establishment of Braganza ascendancy at court. Azurara admits that he made use of the writings of Afonso Cerveira when compiling his chronicles, and it seems likely that Cerveira's work may have been a chronicle of the life of Dom Pedro which, after the latters's fall, was conveniently "lost". The Chronicle was, then, written at a highly sensitive period of Portuguese politics and it is clear that it had a political objective.

Second, it is quite obvious to even the most casual reader that the Chronicle was intended to be a panegyric of Prince Henry and that it must have been written with the connivance, or even under the direct instructions, of the Prince and the court. Azurara was a dependent of Prince Henry as he was a commander of the Order of Christ of which Henry was governor. His writings are one of the clearest cases of image-building and propaganda that one can find and they were written, unlike so many other panegyrics, during the lifetime of their principal subject when they could have the maximum political significance.

The third problem associated with the Chronicle is that it was written according to a formula. The events described have been made to reflect a series of chivalrous values that were quite clearly predetermined by the author. However, it is difficult to

imagine any set of ideological garments that are so ill-fitting.
The details of the events described, and the chivalrous gloss
placed on them, are sometimes almost ludicrously out of phase. As
P. E. Russell wrote in 1960, 'Like Froissart, Zurara usually seems
incapable of seeing the contradiction between his general concepts
and the facts he has to narrate.'(2) Yet even Russell ends up by
accepting much of the chivalrous language of the Chronicle at face
value. He closed his 1983 article with the words 'It looks as if
... it was in fifteenth-century Portugal that chivalry was more
enthusiastically used as a guide to political action, and had more
far reaching practical historical results, than anywhere else'(3)

To put it succinctly, the Chronicle was intended to be a
public relations exercise and political propaganda, but because it
is so detailed, and because it appears to provide historians with
so much that they want to know, the propaganda has, over a period
of five centuries, been readily accepted and easily assimilated
into the critical bloodstream.

Azurara's portrait of Henry and his interpretation of
events has, therefore, been largely accepted by generations of
historians, each of whom has added his own gloss to events and
reinterpreted the story to suit the ideological needs of his own
day but, all the time, dancing to the strings that the old
puppet-master tied back in the fifteenth century. Azurara
portrayed Henry as a paragon of chivalry and as a model of the
virtues most admired in the fifteenth century. He combined in his
own person the bravery and devotion of a knight and the chastity,
self-denial and sanctity of a religious. It was he, virtually
singlehanded, who organised the voyages and encouraged the sailors
and captains, and Azurara sets out his motives neatly under six
headings: (i) to find out what lay beyond Cape Bojador; (ii) to
open trade with christian peoples; (iii) to find out how far the
power of the Moors extended; (iv) to find a christian people to
aid him against the Moors; (v) 'to make increase in the faith of
Our Lord Jesus Christ and to bring to him all the souls that
should be saved'; (vi) his horoscope prediction.(4) This image of
Henry has had a unique appeal. It flattered the Portuguese people
by giving them a man of heroic dimensions in world history; it
appealed to the church which wanted to represent the overseas
expansion as a religious crusade; it appealed to the Crown because
it justified the royal monopoly, and to the nobility because it
provided an assertion of their values; and, finally, it has always
appealed to historians because it gives a simple, clear and
personalised explanation of a major historical development.

The durability of Azurara's creation, as P. E. Russell
has pointed out, is due to the fact that a mythical figure or
"culture hero" can take on whatever form a particular epoch may
wish. When men of science were highly respected, Henry became a
man of science, a pioneer of geography, navigational science and
cartography; when the ideal of the Renaissance was in fashion

following Burckhardt, Henry became a perfect example of the "Renaissance Man" — soldier, saint, scholar, scientist, patron of things intellectual. This particular image of Henry has proved remarkably persistent in England. One of the most excessively sycophantic biographies of Henry, that of Raymond Beazley which was published in 1895, was reissued as recently as 1968. However, Prince Henry reached his greatest achievment as a "culture hero" during the Salazar regime in Portugal. He became the historical figure on whom the regime sought to hang its entire ideology — its christian, catholic principles, its civilising mission and its respect for the divine guidance of its rulers. During the Second World War it was popular to portray Henry as the last of the crusaders and in his well-known book, A Cruzada do Infante D. Henrique, published in 1943, Joaquim Bensaude took the worship of Henry to extreme lengths.

> In the Infante Dom Henrique we meet the religious
> vision of a Dante ... [but] ... neither the
> sufferings of Dante, nor those of Milton or
> Beethoven, nor the sixty years of artistic anguish
> of Michelangelo have the tragic grandeur of the
> martyrdom of the Infante, responsible for the death
> of his four brothers and for the devastation of the
> House of Aviz'.(5)

Henry appeared in stone at the head of a procession of navigators and conquistadores on the monument erected to the discoverers at Belem near Lisbon, and the celebrations to mark the quincentenary of his death in 1960 saw whole industries being created to perpetuate the memory of the hero of the New State. The output of publications on Henrician topics became a veritable avalanche, some of them like the Portugaliae Monumenta Cartographica being of truly monumental proportions.

Academic historians have, on the whole, accepted the close relationship which Azurara established between the events of the life of Prince Henry and the origin of modern European expansion. The classic statement of Portuguese academic opinion is probably that of Jaime Cortesão, who was chosen to write the chapter on the discoveries in Damião Peres nine volume História de Portugal.(6) In his chapter Cortesão brought together all the theories he had spent his life elaborating and in these can clearly be seen a deep schizophrenia which is typical not only of Portuguese but of many non-Portuguese historians. While admitting that the expansion was primarily an economic enterprise he then set out to explore a variety of non-economic theories about its origins. He claimed that the Portuguese discoveries were the result of a well-thought out plan to reach India, originating with Prince Henry and carried on faithfully after his death by Afonso V and João II. Every aspect of Henry's life fitted the plan: the attack on Ceuta was to gain knowledge of the African interior; Madeira and the Canaries were to be settled as supply bases and

way-stations; nothing was allowed to stand in the way of the
steady realisation of the grand strategy of reaching India. When
there are periods in which it appears that nothing much is
happening, this is because of the "policy of secrecy" which led to
the systematic suppression of details about the voyages and the
full range of Portuguese activities. Cortesão's theories about
the origins of the discoveries were, of course, irrefutable. They
had infallibility built into them. Once the existence of a
"policy of secrecy" had been accepted then the less information
about voyages that survived, the firmer became the proof of the
existence of a great national plan.

On the whole the primacy of Prince Henry in initiating
and masterminding Portuguese, and hence European, overseas
expansion has been accepted by the leading English-speaking
historians. It is virtually unquestioned by Edgar Prestage whose
Portuguese Pioneers, published in 1933, was reissued in 1966 and
remained the standard work until 1977. Bailey Diffie and P. E.
Russell have done very important work in de-mythologising Henry,
but they too end by accepting the view that a Henrician plan of
some sort existed.

A fundamentally different view of the origins of the
discoveries was developed by the Portuguese historian Vitorino
Magalhães Godinho in a series of publications after the Second
World War.(7) Godinho did much of his work in Paris where his
doctoral thesis was published in 1958. He was very much part of
the annaliste school and never belonged to the Portuguese academic
establishment. His views were profoundly unacceptable to the
Salazar regime and, on the whole surprisingly, they have proved
unacceptable to most non-Portuguese historians as well. None of
Godinho's major works have appeared in English and there is no
clear statement of his views in any English publication, though
the reader can get a fair picture from the few pages of Oliveira
Marques' History of Portugal that deal with the discoveries and
from Pierre Chaunu's European Expansion in the later Middle Ages.

Godinho placed the Portuguese "discoveries" firmly in
the context of the fifteenth century Mediterranean economy and the
political and economic history of Portugal. He stressed the
evolution of Portuguese society, the bullion crisis of late
fourteenth century Europe, the rise of sugar cultivation, the
decline of wheat farming and the close commercial links with North
Africa. He stressed also the role of the bourgeoisie in
establishing the Aviz dynasty and their backing of João I and Dom
Pedro. Finally he elaborated the theory that the exploration of
Africa was really the work of Dom Pedro and his followers,
although Henry became the main beneficiary of the expansion.

This article seeks to present English readers with a coherent picture of the origin and nature of Portuguese expansion making full use of Godinho's ideas.

The Discoveries in their setting

During the fourteenth century Portugal and Castile had been drawn into the Hundred Years War. English and French armies intervened in the peninsula, battles were fought at sea, and John of Gaunt had tried to establish his claim to the Castilian throne. Attempts to unite the Portuguese and Castilian crowns through royal marriages continued to be made and proved attractive to sections of the Portuguese nobility who themselves often had marriage connections with Castilian nobility or who belonged to one of the military orders - Calatrava or Santiago - that were Castilian in origin. For the Portuguese nobility, as for their English and French contemporaries, war was a form of honourable employment, a way of maintaining one's status and a means of enrichment through plunder, ransoms, the acquisition of lands, commanderies in the military orders or offices.

The importance of military employment for the Portuguese nobility was enhanced by their economic situation. During the fourteenth century the problem of the concentration of land in the hands of the church and of the great nobles was beginning to occupy peoples' minds. Rents were ceasing to keep up with the profits of trade and the long emphyteutic leases on which land was held meant that rent adjustments were infrequent and the land market could not adapt to changing conditions. Large tracts of land went out of cultivation and minor nobles who had no patrimony sought maintenance in the entourage of the great. The system of conthias had existed since the thirteenth century by which nobles were paid a retainer by the Crown or by some other great man and in return served him in a military capacity.(8)

Although the independent Moorish kingdom of the Algarve had been extinguished in the thirteenth century, the Hundred Years War had revived the expectations and patterns of behaviour of the reconquista. Wars in pursuit of shadowy dynastic claims ravaged the frontier regions and Castilian galleys attacked shipping and the coastal communities. These wars coincided with and clearly contributed to the demographic decline of the fourteenth century and helped create a deep economic crisis. The Portuguese historian, Verissimo Serrao, has written, 'It is an accepted fact that the countryside was largely deserted in the time of Dom João I'. That there was extensive rural depopulation due to war and plague is also the conclusion of H. B. Johnson who has studied the returns of the royal inquiry of 1395 into agricultural production and tax paying capacity.(8) Gold and silver coinage almost disappeared and only Moroccan coins sometimes circulated, exchanged for the fruit sent across the straits of Gibraltar from the Algarve. This shortage of bullion was a problem affecting the whole of western Europe and its root cause lay in the adverse flow of silver via Venice and the other Italian cities to the East. The converging problems of the spread of wastelands, the growth of vagrancy, the drift of population to the towns and periodic food shortages, were particularly difficult to comprehend as they appeared to be contradictory trends. However, they were problems which deeply concerned the rulers of fourteenth century Portugal and the Lei das Sesmarias of 1375 was passed to try to bring some of the wasteland back into cultivation by allowing tax-free occupation on short term leases. The chronic insecurity of the wars, however, defeated all attempts to legislate people back onto the land.

On the death of King Fernando in 1383 civil war broke out with factions of the nobility backing the Castilian claimant and supporting a Castilian invasion of the country. The rival faction of the nobility gathered round the figures of the Master of the Order of Aviz and the Constable, Nun'Alvares Pereira, himself the object of a chivalrous legend as exaggerated as Henry's own. These men successfully mobilised popular support in the capital, which they happened to control, and called urgently for English intervention. A combined English and Portuguese army then won the battle of Aljubarrota which enabled the Master of Aviz to claim the throne. Historians have always seen Aljubarrota as the decisive moment in the history of Portugal when merger with Castile was finally defeated and the country's independent destiny was secured. With the long view of hindsight this is no doubt true, but the battle did not immediately resolve all the important issues, nor did it prevent the Castilian orientation of much of the Portuguese nobility from reasserting itself on subsequent occasions in the fifteenth and sixteenth centuries. The war with Castile, indeed, dragged on until 1411 with Portugal lending half-hearted support to John of Gaunt's wars in Castile.

The merchant classes had a powerful influence on the new regime and enjoyed a voice at court in the person of the vedor da fazenda, João Afonso, and later the Infante Dom Pedro. Although they had suffered badly in the wars since 1369, it is clear that, since the thirteenth century, there had been a very considerable growth in the wealth and influence of the Portuguese merchant and shipowning class. Portugal had commercial treaties with England and the Netherlands and there was a Portuguese factory at Bruges. Shipowners had negotiated privileges from the Portuguese kings and a system of marine insurance had been initiated. For the merchants further Castilian wars were wholly unprofitable as they laid Portuguese trade under the constant threat of attack by Castilian galleys.

João of Aviz found himself in much the same position as his Lancastrian contemporaries in England. His possession of the throne was due to a coup d'etat and not to a just title. He was

faced with the problem of ending a continental
providing for a quarrelsome class of nobles who w\
unemployed by the outbreak of peace. At the same ti\
pursue policies which would maintain the support o\
classes. It was in this context that in 1412 the \
first began to discuss a policy of overseas expansion.

The North African Policy

It is likely that a number of policy options for
overseas expansion were fairly widely debated. Granada was the
most obvious field for further expansion as it would reawaken the
ideologically acceptable traditions of the reconquista. Gibraltar
was suggested at various times as a limited objective, as were
other targets in the Mediterranean, but all of these ran the risk
of awakening the hostility of Castile. Eventually the decision
was taken to launch an attack on Ceuta on the Moroccan side of the
straits of Gibraltar. In 1415, the year of Henry V's invasion of
Normandy, the city fell into Portuguese hands.

The attack on Ceuta was to be the beginning of a century
and a half of Portuguese wars in Morocco, wars which gradually led
to most of the Moorish towns on the Atlantic coast being captured
by the Portuguese. In 1458 Alcacer was taken and in 1471 Arzila,
Larache and Tangier. Agadir was taken in 1505, Safi in 1508,
Azamor in 1513 and Mazagão in 1514. Initially the idea of
expansion in Morocco had very wide support in Portugal. Morocco
was known to be rich agriculturally (Godinho claims that it was
especially famous for its corn lands and sugar production though
C. R. Boxer is sceptical of this) and to be a centre for the
production of fine cloths and the breeding of horses. It was also
known that the West African caravan routes terminated on the
Moroccan coast and these brought gold, slaves and other exotic
products. In the fourteenth century the Genoese had established
factories in many North African cities (including Fez and Arzila)
in order to tap the African caravan trade. Through their agents a
reasonably accurate picture of the Niger region had been acquired.

The Portuguese policy of expansion in North Africa,
therefore, initially had the support of the merchant community
which was keen to establish itself in the Moroccan port cities to
the exclusion of the Genoese. Godinho has shown that their
expectations were not entirely false, for Ceuta proved a
profitable area for Portuguese commerce at least until the 1440s,
and the trade in gold enabled Portugal to begin the revision of
its currency in the 1430s.

However, the North African policy had an appeal also to
the nobility (it was this dual appeal to merchants and nobility
that so commended the attack on Ceuta in 1415) and it was an
appeal that was to prove lasting. North Africa was close at hand

and relatively easy of access. It provided opportunities for the
nobility to hold commands and to perform feats of arms which would
establish their reputation and help maintain their status.
Service in Africa could also earn them rewards from a grateful
sovereign. The Duke of Braganza, for example, secured the status
of a city for the town of Braganza in reward for the services he
had rendered in Africa.(10) However, many of them also believed
that North Africa could be conquered in the same way as the
Iberian peninsula had been and that lands, seigneuries and servile
populations could be acquired. Many of them did indeed acquire
lands and titles to land in the neighbourhood of the fortified
towns in Morocco. However, in the long term the expansion of
Iberian settlement across the straits did not materialise. It
proved impossible to revive the sustained military effort of the
reconquista and it is significant that the military orders, which
had originally been founded to carry on the war against the Moors,
objected to a papal plan put forward in 1456 to establish houses
in North Africa and to concentrate their efforts in the new field
of endeavour.(11)

Among the reasons why the new reconquista failed was the
fact that the nobility found it much more attractive to use the
fortress towns as bases for piracy. Their piratical activity took
place both on land and at sea. On land they mounted raids into
the Moroccan heartland to obtain plunder and to make captives, who
could be sold as slaves if they were poor or who could, much more
profitably, be ransomed if they were men of substance. Such raids
could equally well be mounted at sea and the capture of Moorish
ships and raids on the Moroccan coast became a favourite pastime
for Portuguese fidalgos. It is clear that, in the long run, this
type of raiding and piracy would not lead to permanent conquest
and was inimical to the establishment of peaceful settlements.
The practice of harrying the countryside round the fortress towns
destroyed any possibility that it might provide food for the
garrisons. Instead food had to be imported and the supply of the
fortresses became a major preoccupation of Portuguese policy.
Agreements had to be made with Castile and Brittany to secure
adequate imports of grain.

All his life Henry was a keen advocate of the Moroccan
policy and it was with the Moorish wars that his contemporaries
chiefly associated him. The carefully constructed panegyrics of
Azurara make Henry the key figure in the capture of Ceuta, in the
defence of the city in 1419 and in the disastrous expedition to
Tangier in 1437 which he commanded. Even if Henry was not, in
fact, the mastermind behind these policies, it is significant that
his chronicler wished it to be thought that he was. For the early
1450s, when Azurara was writing, was a period when fresh Moroccan
expeditions were being planned.

Soon after 1415, however, the Moroccan policy ceased to
represent a national consensus, and the rival interest groups

seeking to control Portuguese policy expressed their hostility in an increasingly ideological way. It has been pointed out that the chronicler, Fernão Lopes, who recorded the rise to power of the Aviz dynasty, was no lover of the old nobility nor a believer in their chivalrous pretensions.(12) The same appears to have been true of the Infantes Pedro and João. When the expedition to Tangier was under discussion, these two opposed the whole idea on the grounds that the country was too poor and depopulated, that it was not in the national interest and that to kill Moors, in what would be an unjust war, was not doing the will of God. Pedro and João were clearly articulating the views of the merchant classes who were their supporters and who were opposed to pursuing a policy of conquest of which the nobles would be the main beneficiaries. Henry and the youngest of the five brothers, the Infante Fernando, on the other hand, became the chief spokesmen of the noble class. (One of the reasons used to justify the Tangier expedition, we are told, was that the Infante Fernando was discontented with the small size of his patrimony and wanted to increase his wealth and powers of patronage.) They represented their interest in terms of chivalrous and crusading ideals. In 1436 Henry submitted a memorial to the king on the matter in which he argued strongly for the traditional view that an attack on the Moors would serve God and be to the honour of the participants (although Godinho thinks the most significant aspect of this "Estremoz memorandum" is the fact that Henry actually mentions bodily pleasure and temporal gain as among the legitimate objectives of life).(13)

So deeply committed was Henry to the Moroccan policy and to the ideology that had been employed to justify it that, after the disastrous defeat at Tangier, he found himself in the position of having to argue against the ransom of his captured brother for whom the Moors demanded the surrender of Ceuta. The exaggerated use of the language of chivalry in Azurara's chronicle is not, therefore, to be explained by the fact that this represented values universally acknowledged in his day, but by the very opposite – the fact that these values were being challenged by powerful interest groups opposed to the pretensions of the nobility. Chivalry was used by Azurara as the manifesto of a party at court and it is not therefore surprising that the naked interest of this party shows so clearly through the rather thin chivalrous veneer on almost every page.

The Origins of the African Voyages

At the end of the fourteenth and beginning of the fifteenth centuries, the Portuguese fidalgos and escudeiros (squires) became increasingly involved in piracy to earn a living and maintain their status. Vessels would be commissioned by one of the great nobles and captained by a fidalgo of his household. These would then cruise in the straits or off the Moroccan coast in search of prizes. Plunder, slaves and ransoms were the objective of these cruises and the great Portuguese nobles maintained their own _alfaqueques_ to arrange the ransoming of prisoners. Like his contemporaries Henry commissioned _fidalgos_ of his household to cruise for prizes. Gonçalo de Sintra, for example, was a man 'who had ofttimes sailed in the ships of the armada by his lord's command and had taken part in very great actions, both on the coast of Granada and Ceuta'. Gonçalo Pacheco, one of the prince's retainers, 'always kept ships at sea against the enemies of the kingdom'. João Goncalves Zarco and Tristão Teixeira were sent on a 'warlike enterprise against the Moors' instead of which they went to explore Madeira. Others were busy cruising as well. Mafaldo, who accompanied Goncalo Pacheco, was described as a man 'who had been many times in the Moorish traffic' and was owner of his own boat, while Zarco and Teixeira were accompanied by Bartholomew Perestrello (the future father-in-law of Columbus) who was a member of the household of the Infante João. In 1463 Rui Valente described as _cavaleiro da casa real_ and _provedor da fazenda do Algarve_ (which suggests he had been one of Henry's retainers) armed a caravel to cruise against the Moors in the straits receiving from the king a fifth of the proceeds of the prisoners ransomed.(14)

It is the activities of Henry's privateers that have been seized on by historians as the first "voyages of discovery". In chapter VIII of the _Chronicle_, Azurara explains how Henry's captains year after year failed to round Cape Bojador because of their fears of what lay beyond, but he then naively goes on to say that 'they did not return wholly without honour for ... some made descents upon the coasts of Granada and others voyaged along the Levant seas where they took great booty of the Infidels with which they returned to the kingdom very honourably'. Godinho expressed it succinctly when he wrote, 'Almost all, if not all, the voyages promoted by the Infante up to 1434 must have been corsair expeditions which Zurara subsequently transformed into attempts to round Bojador'.(15)

It should be emphasised at this stage that there was no mystic Cape Bojador round which mariners dared not sail. From the late thirteenth century there had been regular voyages down the Atlantic coast by Genoese, French, Catalan, Castilian and Portuguese vessels, and no doubt Moorish vessels as well. The Canary islands were frequently raided for slaves and ships almost certainly traded as far south as the kingdoms of the Senegal region - or so P. E. Russell interprets a crucial passage in the French chronicle of the Canaries. Even Jaime Cortesão admits that when the Portuguese drew maps they made use of the names already well established for the various geographical landmarks.

So Henry's privateers were not sailing into new waters, nor was Henry the first nobleman to interest himself in this region. In 1344 Don Luis de España had been invested by the pope

with the sovereignty of the Canary islands and had every intention
of conquering and settling them. In 1402 a concession to conquer
the Canaries was granted to Jean de Béthencourt, a nobleman of the
court of the duc de Turenne. In 1418 Béthencourt sold his rights
to the Castilian Count of Niebla. All these men organised, or
tried to organise, expeditions to the islands and Béthencourt sent
slave-raiding expeditions to the African coast in 1405 in the same
way that Henry was later to do. Godinho has pointed out how
similar Bethencourt's motives, as reported by his chronicler, are
to those ascribed by Azurara to Prince Henry. Béthencourt is
supposed to have sought the honour of God and the holy faith; his
own profit and honour; the discovery of the lands south of
Bojador; and the extension of his conquest. He is also supposed
to have wanted to contact Prester John via the Rio do Ouro. It
looks as though motives such as these constituted a standard
ideological justification for fairly routine enterprises in
piracy, slaving, trade and settlement.(16)

The early Portuguese "voyages of discovery" therefore
were a natural offshoot from the seizure of Ceuta, and the
development of the latter as a base for privateering attacks of
Moorish shipping. Many noblemen were sponsoring corsairs, but
only Jean de Béthencourt and Prince Henry were fortunate enough to
have any one to chronicle their piratical activities and only
Henry's chronicle succeeded in catching the imagination of
historians.

The Royal Princes and the New Nobility

The reason why the great nobles of Portugal needed to
find outlets for the energies and enterprise of their retainers in
privateering and wars in Morocco needs to be placed in a context.
The wars with Castile had seen a major blood-letting among the old
nobility. Many of them lost their lives in the fighting or threw
in their lot permanently with Castile and were dispossessed after
the battle of Aljubarrota. The supporters of the new regime
stepped into their shoes, received their confiscated estates and
gradually formed themselves into a new nobility closely linked to
the fortunes of the new dynasty. To meet the expectations of his
supporters for rewards, João I (of Aviz) found himself forced to
make major gifts of lands, revenues and jurisdictions and to
alienate much of the Crown's resources. Alienation of royal lands
merely exacerbated the serious decline in royal revenues that
derived from other cuases. In 1395 an inquiry was carried out
into the taxable capacity of rural Portugal and the full extent of
the depopulation and the loss of taxpayers was revealed. In order
to save the royal patrimony from being wholly wasted a decree of
1403 had stipulated that all merces (grants) by the Crown should
only pass in primogeniture and this was confirmed in the Lei
Mental of 1433 by which King Duarte tried to repossess some of the
alienated lands.

The chief beneficiary of these grants was, without doubt, the Constable, Nun'Alvares Pereira, who acquired extensive lands and revenues for himself and grants also for his wife and mother. Others to benefit were the king's immediate relatives. His bastard, Afonso, married the Constable's daughter and later became Duke of Braganza. His sons were endowed with titles and lands and the Braganza inheritance was specifically excepted from the Lei Mental. In 1408 the Cortes voted a large establishment for the Infantes Pedro and Henry who thereafter assumed an important role in the government of the country. Although the major towns had their own form of self-government, the unsettled nature of the Castilian frontier and the sparseness of the population in many rural areas made the responsibility for government the affair of the local nobility.

In practice the country became divided between the royal princes. The Infante Pedro was made Duke of Coimbra and was entrusted with the great fortified stronghold of Montemor. He effectively dominated the north of the country. Henry, in addition to his lordships of Viseu and Covilham, was made governor of the Algarve and controlled the south. The Branzas were strong in the frontier regions. The king also endowed his sons with the properties of the military orders. He himself was Master of Aviz. He made the Infante João head of the Order of Sántiago whose lands lay in the Alentejo, and Henry was made administrator of the Order of Christ, the inheritors of the possessions of the Templars. These included the fortress town of Tomar near Lisbon and extensive lands in the north.

These governorships and endowments gave the princes enormous resources and powers of patronage, enabling them to provide for the sons of the nobility who became their retainers. Throughout their towns and jurisdictions they could appoint to judicial and fiscal offices; they made military appointments in their fortresses and maintained private armies; and they had at their disposal the commanderies of the military orders. At the end of the sixteenth century there were 600 commanderies enjoying an income of 150 contos. These commanderies conferred honour and status, brought with them revenues from the property of the orders and, most important of all, they granted immunity from the ordinary courts of law. At the centre of these great baronial establishments was a princely household or court in which it was still the custom for young fidalgos and escudeiros to receive their education and be provided with career opportunities. Under João II and Manuel retaining on this scale was to be concentrated at the royal court but in the early fifteenth century it was still a function of the great lay and ecclesiastical nobles. Azurara, for example, recounts that

> it was the custom for the Infante [Henry] not to
> give the position of a squire to any youth of his
> court till he had exercised himself in some feat
> of arms: and according to their merit he granted
> them in the future such dignity as he though they
> deserved.(17)

Finding employment and opportunities for their young retainers to
to prove their skills and abilities was a constant problem and was
a major reason why the overseas enterprises in Morocco, in the
islands, and at sea were welcomed by the nobility. In an often
quoted passage, Diogo Gomes specifically makes this point when he
says that Henry was interested in the gold trade of Guinea 'to
sustain the nobles of his household'.(18)

It is remarkable that, with so much potential for civil
strife between the rival princely houses, there should have been
only two serious incidents in the course of the fifteenth century
– in 1449 when Pedro was overthrown by the Braganzas and in 1482
when the king himself personally humbled the Braganza family and
asserted his dominance in the state. The overseas expansion of
Portugal provided for the retainers of the nobility and so
contributed to maintaining the stability of the state, in much the
same way as did the exploits of the Lancastrians in Normandy.

Henry can be seen systematically increasing the extent of
his network of lands, jurisdictions and patronage. To his great
lordships of Viseu and Covilham, he added the governorships of the
Algarve and Ceuta. The latter responsibility led to his being
endowed with the resources of the Order of Christ so that he could
devote the income of the order to the defence of the city. In
addition to offices he continued throughout his life to acquire a
huge variety of monopolies, privileges and concessions. He
obtained a monopoly of soap production in Portugal. He obtained a
tithe for the Order of Christ on sardine fishing and a monopoly of
tunny and coral fishing. He also obtained a monopoly on the
import of dyes and sugar. To these were added extensive
concessions in the field of Atlantic trade.

Throughout his life Henry saw to it that he became the
principal beneficiary of trade and settlement in the Atlantic. In
1431 he had been granted the right to settle the Azores and in
1433 was granted seigneurial jurisdiction in Madeira. In 1439 his
trade from Madeira was granted exemption from customs. Once the
slave trade was established on the coast of Africa Henry
negotiated a monopoly of the whole trade for himself in 1442 and
in 1446 this was extended to include a right to collect the royal
fifth on slaves and bullion. In 1446 Henry apparently tried
unsuccessfully to negotiate seigneurial rights for himself in the
Canary islands from the King of Castile. After Pedro's fall Henry
hastened to obtain confirmation of his previous grants early in
1449. Undoubtedly his greatest coup, however, was to secure from

the papacy the ecclesiastical rights in the islands and other conquests for the Order of Christ.   P. E. Russell has pointed out that together these privileges gave Henry virtually the position of a monarch in the islands and on the Guinea coast.

It is probably no coincidence that these grants were frequently obtained at sensitive moments in Portuguese politics. The accession of Duarte in 1433, the struggle for the regency in 1439 and the accession of Afonso V to personal rule in 1448 were all closely followed by grants made to Henry - no doubt to secure his political support.   It was very likely that the rapid confirmation of all his privileges by Afonso early in 1449 was enough to persuade Henry to remain neutral in the short, but for his brother Pedro fatal, civil war in 1449.   Throughout his life Henry was a successful politician who systematically acquired vast wealth, patronage and power for himself, who maintained a large body of retainers and who sought to exercise quasi-regal powers in the whole North Atlantic region.

Of course, all these aspects of Henry's career were grist to the chronicler's mill.   The Moroccan policy was an inspired crusade; the extension of the rights of the Order of Christ was a sign of evangelical fervour; the pirate raids were disinterested discovery; Henry's political balancing acts, which allowed him to survive the swings of the political pendulum, became an otherworldly abstention from politics; his blunders at Tangier and his determination to stick to his Moroccan policy became evidence that he put God's service above all other considerations. However, these claims should be seen for what they are, the ideological exposition of a career which is perfectly comprehensible in terms of fifteenth century society and which is comparable to the career of many of the great nobles in western Europe at this time.

The Development of Overseas Expansion

While Ceuta and Henry's port at Lagos in the Algarve were being used to mount piratical raids on the Moors, Portuguese expeditions visited and tried to establish settlements in each of the three island groups of the North East Atlantic.   Of greatest interest to the Portuguese were the Canary islands.   The European connection with the Canaries has been well documented by recent historians.   The original attraction of sailing to the islands in the fourteenth century had been slave raiding and regular raids on the Canaries over a period of a century led to the virtual depopulation of four of the islands.   The other islands, Teneriffe, Palma and Grand Canary, remained targets for slavers well into the fifteenth century and Azurara records details of a number of such raids.   Throughout the fifteenth century French, Castilian and Portuguese noblemen quarrelled and fought over the seigneurial rights in the islands but the Castilian sovereignty of

them increasingly went uncontested and was eventually confirmed by
the treaty of Alcaçovas in 1479. The first Portuguese nobleman to
have tried to establish his claim was not Prince Henry but
Fernando de Castro who sent a large expedition in 1424. Prince
Henry tried his luck in 1430 and in 1448 sent an expedition to
enforce his seigneurial rights in Lanzarote. From then until
about 1454 a desultory war took place between Portuguese and
Castilians with Henry's privateers raiding Castilian settlements
and taking Castilian prizes in the waters around the Canaries.
Judging by the number of vessels involved, Prince Henry and his
fidalgos seem to have been much more interested in this corsair
war than in African voyages, and this fits closely the pattern of
Henry's career that has been already noted.

The rivalry of Portugal with Castile is an important
motif underlying the events of the fifteenth century. Godinho has
suggested that the seizure of Ceuta was, at least in part, a
pre-emptive strike against the Castilians establishing a foothold
in North Africa and the same reasons have been used to explain the
other Moroccan expeditions. Castilian ships fished and traded
down the Moroccan coast and rivalry in the Canary islands was
endemic. The fact that the native Canary islanders put up
determined opposition meant that the three largest of the islands
were not occupied till the last years of the century and the
political uncertainty about who would eventually conquer them
served only to stimulate the rivalry of Portugal and Castile.

Portugal's interest in the islands, however, stemmed from
causes other than her participation in slaving, strong economic
pressures were at work. Already at the end of the fourteenth
century the marked economic and social differences between
northern and southern Portugal were making themselves felt. In
the north the long period of christian settlement and the
mountainous terrain favoured the emergence of smallholdings and
tenures which were divided and subdivided between families. This
fact was graphically brought out by H. B. Johnson in his study of
the village of Povoa del Rey in the fourteenth century when two
thirds of the peasant population had sub-subsistence holdings.
Land hunger and overpopulation were keenly felt, impoverishing the
nobility and driving peasants from the land to the coastal cities
or onto the roads. From the north has always come the pressure to
emigrate - a fact that appears to have been as true of the
fifteenth as of the twentieth centuries. In the south the
reconquest from the Moors led to the formation of great estates in
the hands of the nobility, the church and the military orders.
The south became a region with a low population density where
fluctuations in the conditions of agriculture reduced much of the
population to the status of impoverished estate serfs and
labourers. Figures from the early sixteenth century show this
situation graphically. While the two northern provinces of
Entre-Douro-e-Minho and Tras-os-Montes had population densities of
33 and 12.6 persons per square kilometre, the two provinces south

of the Tagus (Alentejo and Algarve) had 6 and 6.9 persons respectively.(19) A situation of labour shortage often existed in the south and it was there, in the fourteenth century, that much land went out of cultivation and food shortages began to be felt.

Early in the fifteenth century the growing of sugar cane is recorded in Portugal in the Algarve and in the valley of the Mondego. Sugar production, which had been known in Moorish times, was probably reintroduced by the Genoese who provided the technology and the finance. Sugar, however, required rich soils and abundant labour and there is evidence that the sugar masters were always looking for new areas in which to expand production.

Thus in the early 1400s there was pressure for new land on which to settle coming from many different quarters — from fidalgos seeking estates, from peasants and from sugar growers — while increased grain production was recognised to be a national necessity. As it became clear that the conquest of Ceuta was not going to lead to the easy acquisition of new land, interest was increasingly shown in the Atlantic islands whose volcanic soils and abundant rainfall made them exceptionally fertile. The settlement of the Canaries had begun in 1402 but proceeded slowly. Madeira and Porto Santo were settled after 1424 and the Azores from 1439. Henry did not pioneer the settlements but, once they were established, he acquired rights from the Crown which enabled him to claim seigneurial dues and fiscal privileges of various kinds over them. The actual settlement was carried out by "captains" who were granted the islands on condition that they brought in settlers, made allocations of lands and saw to the administration and defence of their captaincies. Settlers were not difficult to find and, once the supply of labour was secured, Italian capital began the production of sugar, though the islands were not given over to monoculture and wheat, wine, cattle and other commodities were of equal importance in the early days.

The Discovery of Guinea

Before the 1440s Portuguese expansionist activity was confined to the North East Atlantic and to regions that were well known and where other peoples beside themselves had been active in piracy, settlement and slave raiding. In 1441, however, a period began in which not only was there rapid development of contacts with West African peoples but the Portuguese for the first time opened up regions that had not been visited before. The political circumstances in Portugal had changed radically in 1439. The attempt to take Tangier in 1437 had failed miserably and the Infante Fernando had been left as a hostage with the Moors. The following year the king had died and after a brief struggle Pedro became regent. Almost at once the pace of commercial expansion down the coast of Africa quickened. Between 1441 and 1447 there

were some twenty recorded voyages and Portuguese ships sailed as
far as Cape Verde.

The fact that vigourous commercial expansion and the
first real exploration took place during the regency of Pedro may
be just a coincidence, but it has been strongly argued that it was
the regent himself who gave the impetus for these developments.
Godinho has pointed out that Pedro owed his position to the
support of the cities and the merchant classes whose interests
were no longer served by the heroics of Prince Henry's Moroccan
exploits. Once in power he did everything possible to encourage
commerce and maritime expansion. The evidence for this view is
circumstantial rather than direct. It is known that Pedro
sponsored some of the voyages and that he took an active interest
in the settlement of the Azores. Azurara also recounts that he
offered a prize, in conjunction with Henry, for the captain who
sailed furthest along the coast in a given year. Apart from this,
there is little direct evidence of his involvement. On the other
hand it is undoubtedly the case that once Pedro was removed from
the political scene in 1448 little further interest was taken in
the African voyages and Henry and the court nobles once again
began to pursue their ambitions in Morocco. It must surely be
concluded that the circumstances of Pedro's regency were
exceptionally favourable for those who wished to invest in African
voyages and that the opposition of the regent to North African
adventures ruled these out as a practical alternative. However,
even if prominence is given to Pedro's backing, some further
explanation is required for the truly revolutionary enterprises of
these six or seven years.

The answer lies quite clearly in the pages of Azurara's
Chronicle. It has been pointed out that the early Portuguese
voyages to the African coast were the voyages of corsairs who, if
they failed to make a rich prize of a Moorish vessel compensated
themselves with catching seals or raiding the Canary islands.
Successful raids on the African mainland seem to have been rare,
but in 1441 a captain returned with a saleable cargo of slaves
which he had captured on land and from that time onwards raids on
the coastal settlements became increasingly lucrative.

It is sometimes implied that the return of Antão
Gonçalves and Nuno Tristão to Portugual with a cargo of slaves in
1441 was a singular event which opened a new era in international
relations. However, slaves had been bought and sold throughout
the Mediterranean region since Roman times and were a highly
valued commodity. The main source of slaves was the Black Sea
region and North Africa where they were either obtained by raids
and piracy or, more expensively, by trade. As has already been
shown, the Canary islands were also regularly raided for slaves.
Slaves had been imported into Portugal prior to 1441 and the
demand was particularly strong in the south of the country, which
no doubt explains the public interest which, according to

Azurara's account, greeted the landing of the slave cargoes at Lagos. The news that slave hunting could be profitably carried on along the southern Sahara coast led to a flood of applications for licenses to cruise in those waters. The granting of these licenses suddenly became a profitable activity and Henry petitioned his brother, the regent, for the exclusive right to grant them. In 1442 Henry was given his monopoly of trade and in 1443 added a papal bull in confirmation of the grant. In 1446 he was granted the right to collect the royal fifth on imported slaves.

Through Azurara's Chronicle quite a lot is known of the people who sought and obtained licenses to go slaving. Although some of the captains were men in Henry's service, and although a few of the ships were Henry's, it is quite clear that most of the vessels belonged to other noblemen, to churchmen, to the military orders, to the captains of Madeira, to individual ship owners and to the other Infantes. There was Gonçalo Pacheco, high treasurer of Ceuta, 'who always kept ships at sea against the enemies of the kingdom'; Alvaro Gil 'an assayer of the mint'; Mafaldo, a ship owner who had 'been many times in the Moorish traffic'; Soeiro da Costa, alcaide of Lagos, a professional soldier who had fought at Agincourt; Alvaro de Freitas, commandant of Aljazur which belonged to the Order of Santiago, 'who had made very great prizes among the Moors of Granada'; there was a commander of the king's galleys, servants of the Infantes Pedro and João and captains in the service of João Goncalves Zarco, captain of Madeira; Diniz Dias commanded a caravel belonging to Dom Alvaro de Castro and another captain commanded one belonging to the Bishop of the Algarve.(20)

The crude and nasty business of slaving is clearly described by Azurara though with the exploits gilded over with the trappings of chivalry. Ships' captains and aspiring squires were knighted for deeds such as capturing an old woman after a chase in the sand, and words are put into the mouths of the participants in these raids by which they continually urge one another to greater deeds in the service of God and the Infante. The term 'honour and profit' become a sort of slogan by which actions of all kinds were weighed and judged. The nature of fifteenth century ideas about chivalry are clearly revealed in these passages. Virtually any activity can be considered chivalrous if it is carried on by force of arms. However, "honour" by itself is not sufficient as an objective. As Nuno Tristão is reported to have said, 'I should receive disgrace, holding the order of knighthood as I do, if I gained here no booty richer than this.' The successful knight was the one who achieved wealth and made his fortune by the use of arms rather than by peaceful activity.

It was the process of slave hunting that was directly responsible for the exploration of new stretches of coast. After a few successful raids, the Portuguese found that the local inhabitants deserted their villages and were on the alert for attacks. It was necessary to sail ever further south to find communities that had not already been raided, and which were unprepared for attack from the sea. As Azurara said, 'they now saw it would be necessary to seek other parts, in which there was no knowledge of their arrival'. In this way every expedition had to descend on a fresh section of coast and this speedily took the captains down the thinly populated Sahara shoreline to the Senegal and the Guinea rivers. Here, however, a different situation prevailed. The Mandinga and Woloff peoples of the coastlands of Upper Guinea proved to be formidable fighters and the Portuguese were worsted in a number of encounters. Capturing slaves now became an extremely dangerous occupation and the enthusiasm for valourous deeds of arms rapidly waned among the Portuguese fidalgos. As Azurara himself said, 'their terrible manner of fighting was such as to strike many men of understanding with great terror.' Raiding for slaves ceased altogether and with it the drive to discover new stretches of coastline. With the end of slave raiding, Azurara's interest in the "valorous deeds" of the Portuguese also ceased. He ends his account with these words, 'The affairs of these parts were henceforth treated more by trafficking of merchants than by bravery and toil in arms'.(21)

The coming of age of Afonso V in 1448 and the displacement of Pedro from the regency left the Portuguese court dominated by the Braganza faction. Afonso V's reign has always been seen as one in which the nobility plundered the royal patrimony, extorting lands, offices and titles from the weak king. Fifty-six titles of nobility were created during his reign in contrast to only two which were conferred by his successor. In 1472 the Cortes complained about the granting of titles to those who could not maintain their status. Afonso's reign also saw a revival of the Moroccan enterprises. Soon after Pedro's death at Alfarrobeira in 1449 preparations were made for another major expedition to Morocco. This was delayed somewhat by the European crisis which resulted from the fall of Constantinople to the Turks in 1453 and from the papal attempt to organise a crusade to retake the city. The Portuguese espoused the cause of this crusade not least because it enabled the Crown to raise extraordinary taxation and, incidentally, to issue the famous gold coin, the cruzado. The crusade, however, never sailed and in 1458 the Portuguese expedition was eventually dispatched against Alcacer. Henry, as one might expect, played a large part in the organisation and planning of this expedition. He died soon afterwards in 1460, when already plans were under way for yet another war in Morocco. In 1463 and 1464 three attempts to attack Tangier failed but in 1471 Portuguese luck turned and both Tangier and Arzila fell into their hands giving Portugal virtual control of the whole Tangier peninsula. Shortly after this, war broke out with Castile as Afonso was persuaded to pursue hopeless ambitions for a union of his crown with that of Castile. The war lasted till 1479. Thirty years of dominance by the Braganzas and their noble followers had, therefore, diverted the thrust of Portuguese expansionism back to regions nearer home and returned it to objectives traditional to the ambitions of the military nobility.

The African voyages did not come to a halt after the death of Pedro but for twenty years after his death relatively few of them even attempted to explore new stretches of coastline. Instead the increasingly prosperous trade in gold and slaves was leased out to shipowners, foreign entrepreneurs and syndicates. A factory was established at Arguim and leased to a syndicate of merchants. Trading voyages to the Guinea rivers were licensed by Henry on a basis that is described by Cadamosto. If the trader provided his own ship and trading capital Henry took a quarter of the profits. If Henry supplied the ship, he took half. However, for the most part Henry seems to have employed his own ships in the kind of activities which had always been his prime interest — raiding the Canaries, ransoming moorish prisoners and seal hunting. Italians from Genoa and Venice increasingly appear as entrepreneurs in the trade and it was probably Italians who explored and charted the Cape Verde islands sometime between 1455 and 1460. Castilians also sailed in increasing numbers to Guinea.

Henry meanwhile never lost interest in extending his fiscal privileges and as late as 1458 he obtained the grant of a "twentieth" on slaves, gold, fish and other merchandise to be paid to the Order of Christ, following the papal bull of 1456 which granted the spiritualities in the region to the Order. After Henry's death in 1460 his vast lands, jurisdictions and privileges were inherited by the king's brother Fernando. The latter appears to have taken no significant part in the African trade and continued the policy of leasing it to individual merchants. A few of the nobility maintained a desultory interest but this mostly took the form of sending out speculative voyages to search for new groups of islands in the Atlantic. A contract would be obtained to search for islands with the understanding that the holder of the contract would have seigneurial rights in any that were found. It was a contract of this kind that Columbus wanted to obtain when he came to the Portuguese court in 1483.

It was to one Lisbon merchant that Portugal owed the really revolutionary voyages of discovery. In 1469 Fernão Gomes contracted for the Guinea trade. By the time his contract ran out in 1474 his ships had explored as far as the Cameroons and had opened up the highly lucrative trade with the "Mine" — the Gold Coast. This trade proved so rich that it was to attract the Portuguese crown — in the person of the heir to the throne, the Infante João — to take a wholly new interest in the possibilities of Africa.

The Legacy of the First Half Century of the Discoveries

The first half century of Portuguese expansion was to leave a legacy and impose certain patterns of behaviour on subsequent developments. First, it was the involvement of the nobility in the Moroccan ventures and the piratical cruises and slave raids that had given the non-commercial drive to the expansion. The fidalgos had been willing to undertake operations of a quasi-military nature with a different expectation from merchants. Where merchants could not see that profits were certain enough for them to risk their meagre capital, a fidalgo would be prepared to undertake a much higher level of risk, seeking his reward as much in plunder, ransoms and slaves as in honest merchandise. Moreover many of the fidalgos had the backing of the military orders or of the great nobles who had resources far superior to those of merchants of the period. Fidalgos might also undertake some risk in return for honour and reputation with a view to establishing their standing among their own peers. Portuguese expansion was to be at its most dynamic when the fidalgo interest was combined with strong mercantile incentives. Warfare, plunder, piracy and trade formed a spectrum of activities which could all be undertaken by the same ship's company in different circumstances, and different sections of Portuguese society were attracted to different ends of the spectrum. However, all these activities formed a continuum and Portuguese expansion could never have taken place without the full range of this spectrum being brought into play.

The role played by the Portuguese crown and royal family in the empire is another legacy of the early period. The Portuguese crown had a tradition of active involvement in trade, as Bailey Diffie has made clear. The kings of Portugal owned ships, traded on their own account and actively participated in maritime matters at all levels. It was a natural transition from this to their role in financing and planning overseas expansion. This has often been contrasted with the role of the Castilian monarchs who tended to take a back seat and to limit their involvement to the granting of contracts to the conquistadores and subsequently to trying to impose royal government on them once they had succeeded in the conquest.

This distinction certainly has some validity and the later Portuguese kings, João II and Manuel, certainly tried to direct the financing and planning of the empire. However, as Godinho has shown, the earliest phase of Portuguese expansion is somewhat more complex. The crown was certainly involved in planning and promoting the Moroccan expeditions but much of the rest of the expansion seems to have depended on initiatives taken by merchants and individual noblemen seeking profitable investments and enterprises. The role of the royal family was much more like that of Castile and was often confined to the granting of licenses and the drawing up of contracts, making sure that it received the fiscal benefits from the new discoveries and securing diplomatic recognition of Portuguese claims.

It has also been claimed that, from the end of the 1440s, the Portuguese empire developed firmly as one of trade rather than conquest and that the pattern of trading fort and factory had its origins in the sixteenth century foundations of Arguim and Elmina. The idea of the trading factory on foreign territory was, of course, not new and had been widely used by the Genoese and others in the Middle Ages. Portugal's adoption of the trading factory in Africa, however, was determined rather by the strength of African resistance to slave raiding. The peoples of West Africa were too well-armed and well-organised to be conquered by tiny parties of Portuguese for all their mobility and firepower at sea. The Portuguese early realised that trade would be a more successful way of making their fortune than war. As "trade" replaced "raid" after the 1440s the <u>fidalgos</u> initially lost interest and it was only the spectacular <u>profits</u> of the Mina gold trade and the sudden prospect of reaching India by sea, which the discovery of the eastward trend of the African coast seemed to promise, that attracted the direct participation of the the crown and the nobility once again in the 1480s and 1490s.

One characteristic of later Portuguese imperialism which is clearly visible in the early stages of expansion was the tendency for the empire to feed off itself. If the original impulse for expansion came from <u>fidalgos</u> and ship owners based in Portugal, its continuation was often generated by the new settlements themselves. By the 1440s shipowners from Madeira were already sailing directly to West Africa and it was Madeirans who first established a successful settlement on Sao Miguel in the Azores. Later the exploration of the Atlantic was to be undertaken at the initiative of the Azorean communities. It is well-known that Columbus married into a Madeiran family and derived much of his training and knowledge from the Madeiran seafaring communitiy. The North African markets provided the cloths needed for the expansion of commerce in West Africa and Madeira supplied the grain that was also in demand. Slaves from West Africa found their most ready market in Madeira and sugar masters spread their production from island group to island group becoming the true pioneers of colonisation in the Atlantic with little specific reference to metropolitan Portugal. Madeiran sugar growers established their industry in the Cape Verde islands and then in the Castilian Canaries where Portuguese settlers formed a significant proportion of the early inhabitants. Later sugar was introduced into the Guinea islands, the Spanish Caribbean and Brazil. The capital was locally generated or came from Italy, the labour came from West Africa and the sugar was sold in various European markets. Already there was a tendency for Portugal herself to be cut out of the economic processes of her own empire, deriving profits from the licenses and the leasing

of royal monopolies and only occasionally from the direct
exploitation of these monopolies herself.

Requiem for Henry the Navigator

After the searching analyses of Godinho and other recent
historians little survives of C. R. Beazley's "culture hero" -
Henry the Navigator. Henry the scientist and scholar of the
Renaissance, the founder of the School of Navigation at Sagres,
has been blown away finally on the winds of critical scholarship.
Bailey Diffie has provided a definitive epitaph:

> No contemporary mentions Henry as an inventor of
> astronomical instruments, nor as improver of the
> astrolabe, quadrant or compass, all known before
> his time. Nor does any contemporary praise his
> knowledge of astronomy ... Henry was not learned in
> geography nor was he a mathematician. Those who
> knew him confirmed that he introduced no new
> navigational skills. If he passed long nights in
> scientific reading and quiet meditation, or if he
> was of a contemplative nature, the records do not
> tell us so.(22)

Henry the planner of the discovery of India has also gone as the
records reveal little or no evidence that he ever thought about
India or knew anything about it; Henry the planner of the African
voyages, if he survives at all, is very much subordinate to Henry
the patron of Moroccan expeditions and pirate cruises. Henry the
crusader, religious devotee and paragon of chivalry is still there
in the pages of Azurara's chronicle but those who still want to
believe that this stilted portraiture is real history must first
persuade themselves that the chronicle is not just an elaborate
and stylised exercise in an increasingly archaic kind of biography
and they must convince themselves that the brutal details of slave
raiding which Azurara unblushingly recounts were really the noble
deeds of chivalry that he, equally unblushingly, makes them out to
be.

Henry, of course, remains a key figure in fifteenth
century Portugal. He was a great baron and for forty years one of
the two or three most powerful men in Portugal; he was the wielder
of great patronage and the lord of numerous towns, castles and
jurisdictions; he was governor of the rich and influential Order
of Christ; he was a great monopolist controlling industries and
fisheries; he was a political survivor whose smart footwork
enabled him to keep his balance in the turbulent politics of the
1440s and to emerge from each crisis with enhanced privileges for
himself and for the Order of Christ, privileges that enabled him
to monopolise the trade with Guinea, the collection of royal
taxation and the levying of ecclesiastical dues throughout the

Atlantic settlements. He was the representative of the faction of
the nobility which was firmly set on expansion in the Iberian
peninsula, the Mediterranean and North Africa and who, through his
chronicler, was prepared to give this faction strong ideological
backing as well as practical support. Finally he was a man who
clearly had no interest in women but who enjoyed power and who
assiduously cultivated his own legend in his own lifetime.

Notes

1. Vitorino Magalhães Godinho, A Economia dos Descobrimentos Henriquinos, (Lisbon, 1962), p.1.

2. P.E.Russell, 'Prince Henry the Navigator', Diamante, XI, 1960, p.15.

3. P.E.Russell, Prince Henry the Navigator: the rise and fall of a Culture Hero, Taylorian Lecture, (Oxford, 1984), p.26.

4. Gomes Eannes de Azurara, The Chronicle of the Discovery and Conquest of Guinea, eds. C.R.Beazley and E.Prestage, 2 vols, Hakluyt Society, 1896, 1899, vol 1, chapter 7.

5. Joaquim Bensaude, A Cruzada do Infante D.Henrique, (Lisbon, 1943).

6. Jaime Cortesão, 'A Genese da Expansão Portuguesa' and 'O Designio do Infante e as Explorações Atlanticas', in D.Peres ed. História de Portugal, (Oporto, 1931), vol 3, pp.333-384.

7. Godinho appended lists of his publications to each of his major works. His mature opinions can best be studied in A Economia dos Descobrimentos Henriquinos, op. cit.; Os Descobrimentos e a Economia Mundial, 2 vols, (Lisbon, 1965-71); L'Economie de l'Empire Portuguais au XVe et XVIe siècles (Paris, 1969). He also published Documentos sobre a Expansão Portuguesa, 3 vols, (Lisbon, 1943-56).

8. For the history of the Portuguese nobility and military orders see Henrique da Gama Barros, Historia da Administração Publica em Portugal nos seculos XII a XV, 11 vols, (Lisbon, 1945-54), vol 2.

9. Joaquim Verissimo Serrão, Historia de Portugal, 2nd edition, 6 vols, (Lisbon, 1978), vol 2, p.236.

10. Ibid, p.238.

11. Gama Barros, Historia da Administração, op. cit. p.338.

12. Antonio Jose' Saraiva, Fernaõ Lopes, 2nd edition, (Lisbon, 1965), pp.42-7.

13. Godinho, A Economia, op. cit. pp.105,140.

14. Azurara, Chronicle, op. cit., pp.56-7, 94, 116, 119, 244, 277; V.M.Godinho, A Estrutura da Antiga Sociedade Portuguesa (Lisbon, 1971), pp.73.

15. Ibid, p.32; Godinho, Os Descobrimentos, op. cit., vol 2, p.522.

16. Godinho, A Economia, op. cit. p.97.

17. Azurara, Chronicle, op. cit., p.169.

18. 'ad nutriendum suos nobiles' in Diogo Gomes, De la Première Decouverte de la Guineé, T.Monod, R.Mauny, and G.Duval eds., (Bissau, 1959), p.15.

19. A.C.de C.M.Saunders, A Social History of Black Slaves and Freedmen in Portugal 1441-1555 (Cambridge, 1982), p.42.   R.C.Hoffman and H.B.Johnson, 'Un village portugais en mutation: Povoa del Rey à la fin du XIVe siecle', Annales, 26, 1971, pp.917-940.

20. Azurara, Chronicle, op. cit., pp.116, 152, 214, 262.

21. Ibid, pp.45, 88, 124, 265, 289.

22. Bailey W.Diffie and George D.Winius, Foundations of the Portuguese Empire 1415-1580 (Oxford, 1977), pp.114-5.

The Estado da India in Southeast Asia

JOHN VILLIERS

The Organisation of the Estado da India

Before any real understanding can be gained of the administrative and judicial systems and practices adopted by the Portuguese at different times in their Asian empire, some definition needs to be attempted of the term Estado da India or State of India, which the Portuguese used as a collective name for all their possessions in Asia from the Persian Gulf to the sea of Japan. However, it is difficult to give such a definition, because at no time in its history was a unified mode of government or system of law and administration established for all the Estado da India's constituent parts. Nor was any authoritative formulation ever issued of a political or moral order which could have provided a conceptual basis and theoretical justification for the Estado da India's claims to sovereignty or hegemony over the different oceans, territories and peoples of which it was formed. At no time was any single guiding principle laid down either in a papal bull from Rome, a royal decree from Lisbon, or a viceregal edict from Goa, which could in some manner be applied to all the different forms of political relationship that the crown of Portugal, through its servants, established with local rulers during the course of the Portuguese imperial adventure in Asia. The gradations of vassalage and suzerainty, the obligations incurred by treaty, the degrees of legitimacy claimed or established by military conquest, the commercial agreements and defensive alliances are as bewildering in their variety as the enormous geographical extent and diversity of the Estado da India itself.

The jurisdiction of the Estado da India extended at one time or another from Sofala and Hormuz in the west to Ternate and Macao in the east. But within this vast maritime area it never succeeded in acquiring any political homogeneity, and it remained little more than a scattered and often inchoate confederation of territories, military and commercial establishments, individuals, goods and interests, administered, controlled or protected, directly or indirectly with varying degrees of completeness by the Portuguese crown or by others on behalf of the crown. Indeed, there were some places in the area that, in spite of being in practice under Portuguese jurisdiction, were not formally considered to belong to the Estado da India at all. A notable example of this is afforded by the several fortified settlements maintained by the Dominicans in Solor and elsewhere in the Lesser Sunda Islands, which were not listed as possessions of the Portuguese crown until 1681, almost a century after the appointment by the viceroy of the first captain of Solor.(1)

The identity of the Estado da India did not therefore depend ultimately on any definition of its territorial limits, because it began as a maritime enterprise and remained so, never exercising direct control over more than a few small enclaves of territory. Its claims to sovereignty were based not upon any hegemony it might gain over areas of land and their populations, but upon its mastery of the open sea and dominance of the shipping lanes that linked those lands together. Indeed, it is perhaps better defined not as an empire at all in the sense that the contemporary Spanish empire was or the Dutch and British empires later became, but rather as an enormous commercial network connecting various points at which trading posts (feitorias), fortified strongholds (fortalezas) or, more rarely, fully fledged urban settlements with their own institutions of municipal government (cidades) had been established. In this respect, the organisation of the Estado da India owed much to the model of the earliest feitorias set up by the Portuguese abroad in the late Middle Ages. Since from the outset the whole of Portugal's trading enterprise overseas was based, unlike the Spanish, on state capitalism, that is to say on the government not merely licensing and regulating the trade but actually conducting it, the feitor acted as the commercial agent of the crown and so in practice also as the king's ambassador, and the feitoria of which he was in charge was in a real sense identical with the Portuguese community in the place. The early feitorias, which were established in those places in Europe, notably Bruges and Antwerp, where the Portuguese had important trading interests, were later founded at several points on the coast of Africa as the Portuguese gradually worked their way southwards to the Cape of Good Hope and into the Indian Ocean. The first feitoria to be set up in India was at Calicut in 1500. In Lisbon the Casa da Guine, Mina e India acted as a clearing and accounting house for goods received from overseas, and its feitor (later known as provedor) was an important crown official and adviser on the affairs of the empire.(2)

The Estado da India may also have owed some of its characteristics as a commercial network, at least in Southeast

Map 1 South-East Asia

Asia, to the earlier trading empires of an only quasi-territorial
nature that had preceded it in the region. Still evident to the
first Portuguese to venture into Southeast Asian waters was the
precedent of the Javanese empire of Mojopahit, which in the
fourteenth century had attained power and prosperity, both by
developing its capacity as a major producer and exporter of rice
and by gaining control of most of the important trade routes in
the Indonesian archipelago, and which yet had only exercised a
very tenuous suzerainty over the more distant parts of its island
realm. The last recorded ruler of Mojopahit, Pati Udara, sent
envoys to Afonso de Albuquerque in Malacca in 1512 to enlist his
support against the Muslim port sultanates on the north coast of
Java. An even more immediate example was afforded by Malacca
itself, which the Portuguese captured in 1511 in order to gain
control of the valuable international trade of which it was then
the leading entrepot and emporium in Southeast Asia and to which
it owed its wealth and importance. It is, however, unlikely that
the Portuguese adopted the practice of commercial expansion ,
without territorial conquest or subjugation of indigenous
populations and without attempting to take control of the means of
production, in conscious imitation of these earlier states. They
seem rather to have striven to follow the example of their
contemporary trading rivals in the area. The only essential
differences, indeed, between the Portuguese and the Malays,
Javanese and other peoples who participated in this Southeast
Asian trading network at the time the Portuguese arrived was that
they were not Asians and that they were concerned solely with the
circulation and exchange of goods and not at all with their
production.

In the Atlantic Ocean the Portuguese were voyaging in
'seas never previously navigated' (mares nunca doutrem navigados),
where they had no commercial rivals and could create their own
trading network without damaging anyone else's interests. Not so
in the Indian Ocean and the Indonesian archipelago, where they at
once encountered both the commercial rivalry and the religious
antagonism of the numerous Muslim peoples with whom they had
perforce to deal. It was this that gave the Portuguese trading
empire in Asia its essentially military character, and
paradoxically made the fortaleza an institution more
characteristic of it than the feitoria.

However, initially there were no plans for founding a
territorial empire by force of arms. Profitable trade was the
first aim and to achieve this the Portuguese depended upon the
goodwill and cooperation of local rulers. It was thus an
essential element of Portuguese policy to establish friendly
relations with these rulers and to win the obedience of their
subjects, as far as possible by peaceful means. The instructions
given in 1506 to D. Francisco de Almeida, first governor and
viceroy of India, make this point very clearly. Almeida was told
to set up a fortress in Malacca but to avoid conflict with the

local people and to explain to them that the fortress was solely for the protection of the Portuguese and their merchandise and not built with any warlike intent. He was instructed to send ships thence to Sumatra, 'which is near Malacca and said to be a very rich island,' and to 'the island of cloves and other important islands adjacent to it, which we are informed are very rich and from which much profit can be derived.' He was to sound out the position of these islands and do whatever he deemed necessary as a mark of possession (that is, set up a padrão or commemorative pillar with the royal arms and a cross on top) and to try to 'subjugate and bring to our obedience the kings and lords of the islands, make them our tributaries, and agree with them on how this can best be done for our service.'(3) Three years later, when Afonso de Albuquerque was planning to attack Malacca, he proposed an alliance with the king of Ayuthya, to whom he offered sovereignty over the territories ruled by the sultan of Malacca if the attack was successful, since the Portuguese themselves only wished to utilise it as a commercial centre and military and naval base. Ayuthya showed no interest in this offer, so Albuquerque went ahead alone and took Malacca unaided. Nevertheless, after the conquest of the city he did nothing to subdue the rest of the sultanate or to dispossess its ruler.(4)

This apparent absence of any intention by the Portuguese to achieve territorial dominance, in spite of a lingering desire still cherished by many fidalgos to perform heroic deeds of knightly valour against the Infidel, is in marked contrast to the carefully formulated and clearly enunciated policy of conquista y reducción pursued by the Spanish in their empire, both in America and Asia.(5) The pragmatic Portuguese evidently soon realised that such an objective was neither necessary nor feasible. Certainly by the time they had reached Malacca and sailed into the waters of the Indonesian archipelago beyond, they seem to have been content to pursue purely commercial ends. King Manuel's famous and grandiloquent title of 'Lord of the Conquest (Conquista), Navigation and Commerce of Ethiopia, Arabia, Persia and India' accurately describes how the Portuguese viewed their imperial enterprise and their notion of its ultimate aims. The 'navigation and commerce' speak for themselves; the 'conquista' clearly meant something rather different to the Portuguese in the context of their imperial policy than it did to the Spanish. For it referred not to territorial conquest, but to a right of sovereignty derived from any legitimate act of acquisition; this could as well be by treaty, or even by purchase, as by force. The assertion by force of such a right of sovereignty was only deemed to be legitimate where, as in Portugal itself in the Middle Ages, lands that had formerly been Christian were held by the infidel and could therefore be taken back by reconquista, or where, as in parts of Muslim Southeast Asia, freedom to preach Christianity or engage in peaceful trade was denied. The Livro das Cidades e Fortalezas of 1581 puts the position succinctly enough:

> When recently the Portuguese, by crossing this
> our sea (este nosso mar) discovered the East
> Indies, they came there with peaceful and not
> warlike intentions towards the rulers and peoples
> of those parts, signifying to them that they
> sought nothing from them but friendship and
> commercial relations.... However, in those places
> where we were ill-received and all kinds of peace
> and trade were denied us we took up arms and,
> having conquered them by force, placed them under
> our rule...(6)

The numerous treaties of peace and commerce concluded between the Estado da India and different Asian rulers proved by their existence that the Portuguese fully recognised the legitimacy of those rulers and their right to rule, and show that they did not seek to overthrow them and incorporate their sovereign territories into the Estado da India.

On sea, however, the situation was rather different. Grotius' principle of mare liberum, which was in general concordance with the principles of natural law as embodied in canon law and to which Southeast Asian rulers, notably the sultans of Makassar, generally adhered, was quite openly rejected by the Portuguese in Asian waters. The whole of the maritime area of the Estado da India was declared to be mare clausum by right of quasi possessio by the Portuguese crown. This provided the sole legal justification for the cartaz system, whereby every Asian trading vessel had to purchase a pass or cartaz from the Portuguese authorities, in return for which it qualified for Portuguese protection. Each cartaz stated the size of the ship, listed her crew and gave particulars of her captain. It also described the cargo and stated for which port the vessel was bound. Every ship had to pay dues on her cargo at the fortaleza or feitoria where the cartaz was issued and to leave a sum as security for the payment of similar dues on her return. Certain goods, notably spices and pepper, iron, copper and naval stores, were prohibited, as was giving passage to Turks and other Muslims. Any ship that was found to be sailing without a cartaz or that violated the terms of the cartaz was automatically confiscated and her crew either killed or sent in slavery to the galleys.

Though the sum charged for the issue of a cartaz was only nominal, the cartaz system was in reality little more than a device to create another source of income by offering opportunities for the diversion of trade to ports that the Portuguese controlled. It was essentially a practical measure and, though the mare clausum principle was adduced to justify imposition of the cartaz system on the shipping of independent sovereign states in Asian waters, it was not considered to imply that the Portuguese had any kind of political hegemony over those states. In so far as the system required any justification or legitimacy other than the capacity of Portuguese sea-power to impose it, it was given this by a series of papal bulls, notably Romanus Pontifex of Nicholas V, promulgated in 1454. It was in any case only effective in the waters round the few ports where the Portuguese were sufficiently in control for such protection to be guaranteed and where they could provide a cafila or convoy, as they did, for example, on the west coast of India for ships sailing from Goa to Gujarat or to the Malabar coast.(7)

Nevertheless, some form of political dominance, however, limited, often followed in the wake of the establishment of trading relations, and attempts were sometimes made to define these relationships in the commercial treaties which the Portuguese concluded with local rulers. Where no treaties were made or where the Portuguese were given no more than a simple right to trade along with the merchants of other nations, it was not possible for them to entertain any pretensions to exclusive control (senhorio) over trade and navigation, let alone to full sovereignty over territory. Such sovereignty could only be exercised over those lands which had been formally incorporated into the Estado da India, either by conquest or by treaty, and were therefore designated as a possessao of the crown. Goa and Malacca belonged to this category of possessões claimed by right of conquest, and numerous places in India, Ceylon and Burma were styled thus following the conclusion of a treaty.(8) In some places the ruler was converted to Christianity and bequeathed all or part of his realm to the Portuguese crown in his will. An example of this was king Tabarija of Ternate, who was converted to Christianity in Goa in 1537, taking the name of Dom Manuel. At his baptism, he donated 'the islands and lands of Ambon and Seram ... from Buru as far as the Papuas', over many of which his own authority was somewhat tenuous, to his sponsor Jordao de Freitas. This donation (doaçao) was confirmed by king Joao III in 1543. The following year, Jordao de Freitas became captain of the Moluccas and, as soon as he arrived in Ternate, he sent his nephew Vasco with two kora-kora to Ambon to take possession. Jordão's intention was, after completing his term as captain, to settle permanently on Ambon and, as lord of it, to convert all its inhabitants to Christianity. He had brought Manuel with him from Goa to take possession of his kingdom but Manuel died suddenly in Malacca on the way. However, Manuel had first made a will naming the king of Portugal as his heir, in order to avoid the kingdom falling into the hands of his Muslim half-brother, Hairun. Freitas went on to Ternate, arrested Hairun and sent him to India, and, having calmed the fears of the Muslims by assuring them there would be no forcible conversions, made them swear allegiance to him as representative of the king of Portugal. He did not enjoy his position for long. In October 1546 the viceroy, Joâo de Castro, sent Bernaldim de Sousa and Hairun to Ternate with a decree (alvará) declaring that Hairun was the rightful ruler of Ternate and that Sousa was to be captain of the Moluccas. Freitas was deposed and sent back to India to defend his position over

Manuel's will and the arrest of Hairun two years before. Ambon's vassalage was, however, confirmed by King Sebastiao in June 1574 to Gonçalo de Freitas, Jordão's eldest legitimate son. (9)

Occasionally, local rulers submitted voluntarily to Portuguese suzerainty, a means of attaining possessão that was generally considered to be highly desirable and which the Portuguese were enjoined to try to achieve by the bull Ineffabilis et Summi Patria of Pope Alexander VI. Such acts of voluntary submission were made by a number of petty chiefs (liurai, régulos) in Timor who had been converted to Christianity. In Ternate in 1514, Tabarija's predecessor, Boleife wrote a letter in Malay to King Manuel I offering him his 'obedience and esteem' and surrendering the island of Ternate and its port with all that was in it to the king of Portugal, 'who may guard and supply it as his own', while Boleife and all his subjects would be vassals of Portugal for all his life and the lives of his successors, 'because there is no monarch under the stars to equal his Highness'. In 1544 Tabarija's successor Sultan Hairun, although a Muslim, declared that he intended to live and die in the service of Portugal, 'not as a man of the Moluccas and king of this country but as a vassal and good Portuguese, of which time will bear witness.' This declaration did not prevent Hairun from later becoming an implacable enemy of the Portuguese.(10) In Ternate and Ceylon local assemblies of notables (known in Indonesia as bicara) were convened somewhat in the manner of the Portuguese Cortes to give their consent to these acts of submission and to legitimate the potential right to hegemony implicit in the Portuguese presence and in the notion of conquista, whether or not any armed conflict had taken place.

The majority of the fortalezas and feitorias of the Estado da India, however, were in places where the Portuguese exercised neither sovereignty in theory nor hegemony in practice. Cochin, Calicut, Chaul, Solor, Ternate were no more than links in the Portuguese maritime network of trade and communications, existing, often precariously, as small oases of Portuguese administration in the midst of the indigenous societies around them. Only in a few places was any formal agreement ever concluded with the local ruler; in most the maintenance of a Portuguese presence depended entirely upon the tacit consent of the local ruler and the goodwill of his subjects, which all too often the Portuguese destroyed by their rapacity and cruelty.

Wherever informal arrangements and peaceful cessions of this kind were made it was difficult for the Portuguese to justify the construction of a full-scale fortaleza with a military garrison, and their fortalezas were therefore officially designated as feitorias, provided with fortifications ostensibly only for reasons of defence. We have noticed how this formula was adopted for Malacca before the decision had been reached to take it by force. As the Livro das Cidades defines it, 'in places of most trade and greatest concourse of merchandise', feitorias were to be set up. These were to be paid for from the royal revenues and to be built as strongholds (casas fortes), 'to protect the merchandise and defend the priests and people in the place'. However, in those places where 'we have been ill received and denied any kind of peace or commerce', the feitoria was to be set up not as a casa forte but as a fortaleza, 'by means of which we governed them and kept them in obedience to us'.(11)

In practice both types of fortaleza-feitoria were the same. The government of the Estado da India only exercised full jurisdiction within the walls, and beyond them only to those inhabitants in the surrounding area who had been converted to Christianity. In certain areas, however, such as Mozambique, Timor and some of the eastern Indonesian islands, where there were numerous factions in the local population and rivals for power among the local rulers and chiefs, the fortaleza could also fulfill the role of protector of one side against another and the Portuguese could on occasion exploit these internal conflicts to their own economic, political or religious advantage. In the Moluccas, the rulers of Ternate and Tidore both sought Portuguese protection against each other and both invited the Portuguese to build a fortaleza in their territory. According to Jesuit sources, they together proposed in 1513 to António de Miranda de Azevedo that the Portuguese build a fortaleza on the island of Makian, which was then under their joint suzerainty.(12) In cases such as this, the exercise of an informal protectorate could evolve into de jure possession and lead to the assertion of claims to full Portuguese sovereignty and attempts to impose Portuguese administration. This happened in Solor, where from 1585 the viceroy nominated a captain of the bastion of Solor (baluarte de Sollor) and superintendent of the dead (provedor dos defuntos). The first captain was Antonio de Viegas, a casado of Malacca. From 1696 governors of Solor and Timor were regularly appointed by the Estado da India.(13)

More rarely, groups of Portuguese developed into semi-autonomous communities with their own administrative organisation and judicial system in a place that remained entirely outside Portuguese administration. The Portuguese merchant communities of Patani and Makassar provided examples of this kind of 'spontaneous colony', as Thomaz has described it.(14) Likewise Macau, where the Estado da India was only periodically and inadequately represented by the captain-general of the Japan voyage, acquired its own political organisation with the tacit agreement of the Chinese government and became a kind of mercantile republic ruled by the municipal authorities of the Senado da Câmara.(15)

Even in Macau, however, the ultimate authority of the viceroy in Goa was never questioned, and such cohesion and unity as the administration of the Estado da India ever possessed was given by the dependence of all its constituent parts on the viceregal government. Goa was declared to be the 'head and principal seat of the state which the crown of Portugal possesses in the east. The ruler of this state, the viceroy or governor, largely because of the great distances that separated Goa both from Lisbon and from the easternmost parts of the Estado da India and the poor communications between these places, was granted almost unlimited powers by the crown during the three years of his appointment, and his office was therefore regarded as 'the most honourable position that any prince in the world can bestow.'(16)

The Estado da India was first formally established with the appointment of its first governor, Dom Francisco de Almeida, in 1505, seven years after Vasco da Gama had landed at Calicut. During these seven years the Portuguese had become permanently established in India and had acquired a military organisation in support of their commercial and diplomatic dealings. The offices of viceroy and governor were at first separate, but their functions were never distinct and they later came to carry identical powers and to be held by the same person. The viceroy could not pronounce sentence of death or mutilation over any fidalgo without permission from the king and could not on his own initiative hire or dismiss the highest officials in his administration and judiciary, though he could, and frequently did, refuse to instate them and could also suspend them without giving any cause if they failed to perform their duties to his satisfaction. Apart from these relatively minor limitations, his powers were very extensive indeed and for most of the time he could act as an independent sovereign. He had authority to approve or withold all disbursements and transactions made by or for the royal exchequer. He could make war or peace with any of the 'kings and rulers in the Indies and of other regions outside it'(17), and the king of Portugal undertook to confirm and fulfill the terms of any truce or treaty of peace the viceroy might conclude, exactly as if he had done it himself and it had been agreed and signed in his presence. Until the union of the crowns of Spain and Portugal in 1580, all the affairs of the empire were dealt with directly by the king and the Conselho de Estado and there was no special council of the Indies in Lisbon to give authoritative advice on the viceroy's policies and to influence his decisions. The only real curb on the viceroy's power, other than the restraints of custom, was his liability to a judicial investigation, known as a residéncia, at the end of his tenure of office. But even this was seldom carried out or was so delayed as to be ineffective.(18)

From an early date after 1505, the viceroy maintained an advisory council, which was modelled closely on the Conselho de Estado in Lisbon and was composed of the chief military, civil, judicial and ecclesiastical officials in Goa, including the archbishop, the chief inquisitor (after the establishment of the Inquisition in Goa in 1560), the vedor da fazenda (overseer of the revenue department), the captain of the fortaleza, the chief attorney of the Relação (tribunal) and other fidalgos of standing. The decisions of this council were however not generally considered to be binding on the viceroy.

The most important official at the viceregal court after the viceroy himself was the secretary, whose office was one of 'great authority which kings usually bestowed on people of confidence and experience whom they sent from this kingdom to the said parts of India in the company of the viceroys.'(19) One of the most distinguished of the secretaries of the Estado da India was António Coelho Guerreiro, who in 1702 was appointed by the viceroy governor and captain-general of Solor and Timor.(20)

After the secretary came the various officials of the two main sections into which the viceregal administration was divided – the revenue department (fazenda) and the judiciary (justiça). The fazenda was controlled by an overseer (vedor geral), whose post was created in 1549 and who was chief financial officer in the Estado da India. He was assisted by a clerk (escrivão) and numerous subordinate officials, of whom the most important were the treasurer of the city of Goa, the chief factor (feitor), the magistrate responsible for the customs (juiz da alfândega) and the officers of the exchequer (casa dos contos) under a chief superintendent or purveyor (provedor mór), who, before the creation of the office of vedor, had been chief financial officer in the viceregal administration. The customs house was headed by an almoxarife, who was directly responsible to the vedor.

The Portuguese generally tried as far as possible to avoid disruption of local commercial activity and conflict with indigenous laws and practices, in accordance with their principle of separation of jurisdictions. Therefore, the majority of the duties and port charges that they levied in Goa, Malacca and the other places where they exercised full authority were kept as close as possible to those previously imposed by the indigenous administrations that they replaced.

There were, as a result, wide variations in the fiscal system between different places in Portuguese Asia. In Malacca, for example, the Portuguese maintained themselves almost entirely from customs revenues, and scarcely any taxes were levied, even though Malacca's food supplies came almost entirely from abroad. This was partly because of the control exercised by the large and powerful Javanese community in Malacca over the rice trade with Java. In Goa, on the other hand, many different taxes were imposed to meet the very high costs of maintaining the viceregal household and government.

Justice in Goa was carried out by a tribunal called, like the supreme court of justice in Portugal, the Mesa da Relação, which was created in 1544. At first this court had only two judges (desembargadores, ouvidores) but this number was increased

to five in 1548 by an order (regimento) of Joao III and again to
ten in 1587. The Mesa da Relaçao was the only court that could
overrule the decisions of captains of fortalezaas and of local
courts. There were different ouvidores in charge of different
departments, such as the chancery and probate, all under the
ouvidor geral da India or chief justice.(21)

In recognition of the Christian origin of the ethical
principles on which their civil law was based, the Portuguese
always maintained separate jurisdictions for the adherents of
non-Christian religions over whom they had sovereignty. Just as
in Portugal itself the Jewish and Muslim communities had their own
jurisdictions and were subject to their own laws, so in the
Estado da India Muslims (mouros) and Hindus and pagans (gentios)
were generally allowed to remain subject to their traditional laws
and under the jurisdiction of their local leaders. Only converts
to Christianity became ipso facto subject to Portuguese law and
acquired Portuguese citizenship, this being seen as the natural
consequence of adoption of the Catholic faith and not as carrying
any ethnic connotations. Not only mestiços but those with no
Portuguese blood at all could, by becoming Christians, acquire
Portuguese citizenship, thus satisfying Portuguese religiosity as
well as helping to make up for the perennial lack of Portuguese in
the Estado da India.(22)

Thus even in those few places where the Portuguese had
established their own institutions of municipal government and
administration, the surrounding population remained largely
unaffected by the Portuguese presence. Nowhere in the Estado da
India did the Portuguese attempt to replace the indigenous laws by
their own legal codes, as the Spanish did in the Philippines
through the imposition of the encomienda system.(23) Instead,
they preferred to graft onto their system the legal systems and
codes they found in the places where they settled. This was the
principle followed by Afonso de Albuquerque in Malacca. There the
Portuguese merely removed the indigenous ruler of an already rich
and powerful city-state by driving him into exile. Their main
purpose in capturing Malacca was not to create a new Portuguese
city on Malay soil but the far more modest and attainable aim of
acquiring a secure base from which to wrest from their Asian
competitors control of the sea routes in the area and the trade
that passed along them. Dom Francisco de Almeida writing to the
king from Goa in 1508, when the capture of Malacca was still only
being considered as a recourse to be avoided if possible, made
this revealing observation: 'As for the fortress which you have
ordered to be established in Malacca, the more fortressses you
have, the weaker your power will become, for all your power lies
in the sea and, if we are not powerful there, your fortresses will
easily be lost.'(24)

After the conquest of Malacca three years later,
Albuquerque only spent five months in the city. During this time

he constructed a fortress and organised the city's internal administration but made no attempt to subjugate any of the neighbouring rulers. Instead, he set out to establish friendly diplomatic relations with them, especially with those who might be expected to support him in his struggles with the powerful Muslim states that had already demonstrated their hostility to the Portuguese intrusion, and with those whose alliance might bring economic advantages, notably in the spice-producing regions. For this purpose, he sent junks to Pegu, Siam, Java, the Moluccas and Banda, and later to China.(25)

Within Malacca the Portuguese scarcely altered the administrative structure which they had inherited from the sultans. Most importantly they kept the system of separate jurisdictions for the different foreign communities, each under its own shahbandar. They also continued the tradition of giving the posts of treasurer (bendahara) and chief administrator (tememggong), the two principal dignitaries of the sultan's court, respectively to a Hindu Keling (Coromandel) merchant and to a Muslim merchant. The Kelings remained the most influential commmunity in Portuguese Malacca, as they had been under the sultans, and Keling merchants entered into trading partnerships with the Portuguese crown, fitting out ships and acting as commercial advisers to the captains.(26)

The only major innovation brought about in Malacca by the Portuguese conquest was the replacement of a Malay by a Portuguese ruling class, and even this made little change in the social structure and economic life of the city or in its administration and legal system. Nor was there even any fixed or permanent military organisation, although the majority of the Portuguese in Malacca were registered as soldados, unmarried men liable to military service, as opposed to casados (married settlers), and were paid, inadequately and irregularly, by the crown. Most of them therefore had no alternative but to attach themselves to individual fidalgos, who thus acquired their own personal armed retinues.

The Portuguese civil administration in Malacca, as elsewhere in the Estado da India, was rudimentary and makeshift by comparison with the elaborate bureaucracies established by the Spanish in the Phillipines and elsewhere in Nueva Espana. There were not at any time under the Portuguese more than about twenty officials appointed by the crown in Malacca and little distinction was made between merchants and government officials, since everybody - officials, soldiers and even clergy - was associated with trade in one way or another. All could carry goods in the royal vessels up to a certain weight according to their rank and, in spite of frequent prohibitions, many traded on their own account in ships that they fitted out themselves.

The relatively few Portuguese who settled permanently in Malacca, married native women and so became members of the group known as casados. These soon gained considerable wealth and influence through their trading activities and their domination of the municipal council (Câmara), the Misericordia, (the charitable organisation which administered Malacca's main hospital) and the other institutions of government and administration. By 1532 there were about forty casados in Malacca and this number had increased to almost 100 by 1580 and 300 by the end of the century. At the siege of Malacca in 1629, however, there were only 120 casados mentioned as available for military service.(27) Albuquerque had deliberately encouraged the development of this Eurasian population in Malacca, which he hoped would provide a bridge between the Portuguese and the indigenous inhabitants, by offering doweries to native women who married Portuguese and giving to casado couples the dusun or orchards abandoned by the Malay nobility who had followed the sultan into exile.

Not until 1552 was Malacca granted the status of a cidade by João III, and it was only in the reign of his successor, Sebastião (1557-1578), that it received its own administration separate from Goa. From that time the governor, who continued to be appointed triennially, administered criminal and civil justice in Malacca independently and also acted as controller of the royal revenue. However, his jurisdiction was in practice limited by the large number of exemptions from judicial proceedings and punishment enjoyed by fidalgos and other Portuguese of rank, and their privilege of appealing to the viceroy if they were accused of any serious crime or in civil cases involving large sums of money.(28)

The administrative organisation of the viceroy's court in Goa was replicated in smaller and simpler form in Malacca and most of the Portuguese settlements in Asia, whether they were officially described as fortalezas or feitorias and whether or not they were in territories where the Portuguese exercised sovereignty or claimed possessão.

Each fortaleza had a military force, though often only a very small one consisting of a few score men, under the command of a captain, whose appointment, like that of the viceroy, was for only three years and was usually given as a reward for services rendered. In Goa itself the municipality had its own captain, as did all the principal fortalezas on the island. In Macau there was no resident captain, and the post was taken in successive years by whoever had the captaincy-general of the Japan voyage. It was usually the importance and wealth of each fortaleza that determined to whom the captaincy was offered, rather than the merits or qualifications of the different candidates for the post, and the conditions under which it was granted and the size of its emoluments likewise varied considerably from one fortaleza to another. The important captaincy of Chaul, for example, was given

to leading fidalgos with years of service behind them as captains
of vessels and commanders of fleets, and experience of financial
administration in the service of the crown.(29) The captains
exercised both civil and military authority, and were usually
assisted by a governor or constable of the fortress (alcaide-mor),
but the importance which the Portuguese attached to maintaining an
independent judiciary soon led to their judicial function being
given to professional magistrates (ouvidores) assisted by a
bailiff or summoner (meirinho), just as in more important
fortalezas their financial and fiscal duties passed to the vedores
de fazenda or to the feitores. Some fortalezas also maintained a
fleet under a naval captain (capitão-mor do mar) but, even though
the possession of a fleet was considered to be 'the most secure
fortification which this state can have', the post of capitão-mor
do mar seems in most places to have been left vacant for long
periods, presumably because there were not sufficient ships for a
captain to command.(30) In Malacca, for example, the post was
never filled 'except when provided for by the king' and in Ternate
only 'when it may be necessary to have a captain and for him to
serve there'.(31)

Although the crown could make nominations to all these
posts on the military and judicial establishment, as a rule only
the most senior of them were filled in this way, and the viceroy
generally appointed to the subsidiary posts candidates who already
held positions in the administration of the Estado da India, many
of whom were casados.

The feitor was of scarcely less authority and importance
than the captain of the fortaleza. In those places where there
was less commercial activity, such as Ambon, he often also
performed the functions of alcaide-mor, almoxarife and vedor. In
Ambon, indeed, the captaincy itself was officially combined with
the feitor's office by a viceregal decree of 1597, a measure that
testifies eloquently to Ambon's dwindling commercial importance at
the end of the sixteenth century and its consequent inability to
earn enough revenue to warrant maintaining both posts. The office
of meirinho in Ambon appears to have been traditionally filled by
Japanese.(32)

However, the feitor's main task was of course to buy and
sell goods and whenever necessary, to conclude trade agreements,
such as that concluded in 1523 with the orang kaya of the Banda
Islands by António de Brito, who wrote from Ternate to the king of
Portugal:

> I did not write to your Highness about the padrão
> that I have erected in Banda [presumably at
> Leitatam], the most beautiful and the largest
> that can be found, with the arms of your
> Highness, nor of the prices that I have agreed in
> the other letter, which I thought I should send
> you by the quicker Borneo route. These prices

are for the cloves which are brought here and for
the mace and nutmeg that Banda produces. I made
this agreement for always with all the notables
(omens omrados) and shahbandars of the islands,
because there is no king, and they all appointed
me to execute it and agreed that whoever opposed
it should die for it.(33)

The feitor was also charged with a wide variety of duties
connected with navigation and shipping, such as the provision of
naval stores and equipment, victuals and armaments, arranging for
caulking and minor repairs to ships, furnishing vessels for the
loading and unloading of cargo, and supplying boxes and bags for
the packing of goods. In the larger ports such as Goa and
Malacca, which had their own docks (ribeiras), the Portuguese
employed their own specialists to carry out these tasks, usually
working under a superintendent (patrão) and one or more masters
(mestres). In the 1580s the docks at Goa employed 42 people, in
addition to numerous slaves, and these included blacksmiths,
coopers, carpenters, ropemakers and sailmakers. There was also a
chief customs officer (guarda-mor), who was in charge of the
slaves, a quartermaster or storekeeper (almoxarife) and a clerk
(escrivão). The almoxarife presided over the stores of provisions
(almoxarifado dos mantimentos) and the armoury (armazem de
armas).(34)

The post of feitor was generally given, like the
captaincy, to those already employed by the crown (criados del
Rey) or in active service (soldados de serviço). In those places
where the Estado da India did not exercise sovereignty and the
Portuguese enjoyed only the right to trade granted them by the
local ruler the feitoria was generally unfortified. Such were the
feitorias in Banda, Makassar, Martaban and Tenasserim. In these
places, because there was no territory under Portuguese
jurisdiction – not even the small area or praça that in the
fortaleza was enclosed by the walls – and so no governmental
function for the feitor to perform, his role was solely to act as
commercial agent of the crown and was thus more nearly comparable
to that of his predecessors in medieval Europe. In these places
the feitor would collect royal dues from local traders or tributes
from rulers, which he would send to the feitorias of Malacca and
Goa under royal seals.(35)

In the larger Portuguese trading ships sailing in Asian
waters there was also a feitor on board, who traded on the king's
account, though in smaller vessels the captain would fulfil the
feitor's functions. During the long periods of waiting for the
monsoon, described in Portuguese as "wintering" (invernar), the
feitores would disembark and set up an improvised, temporary
feitoria. This was done frequently in the Banda Islands and in
Timor and some of the lesser Sunda Islands, where the
establishment of a more permanent Portuguese presence was

prevented by the hostility of the local rulers or made unnecessary by the small volume of business.(36)

The Portuguese never succeeded in imposing the crown monopoly east of Malacca and only incompletely west of it, so they devised a system of giving licences to individual Portuguese to make trading voyages to different areas. In return for this royal licence the person to whom the voyage had been granted paid to the crown customs duties on his cargo and a percentage of his profits. With the exception of those to Moçambique, Ceylon and the Moluccas, which were carried out by royal fleets, most of these viagens dos lugares were granted to private individuals who had rendered distinguished services to the crown. Initially, the crown either provided the ship or paid a sum of money (usually 3000 cruzados) instead, but in the second half of the sixteenth century the practice grew up of selling the voyage by auction and making the successful bidder fit out and arm a vessel at his own cost. His chief profit from the voyage would be gained by charging freight on the goods that the ship carried and from the return on capital that he invested.(37) The office of provedor dos defuntos was usually also bestowed on the captain of the vessel, and this could be very lucrative, since, as the livro das cidades comments wryly, the 'goods of the dead came belatedly or never into the hands of their heirs.'(38)

In unfortified places where there was provision for a voyage, as for example in the Banda Islands, the captain would also have charge of all the ships in the port of destination and exercise civil and criminal jurisdiction over them, so that 'with this power he has more perquisites than private individuals', and could give himself first choice of cargo and the right to be the first to buy and sell the goods.(39)

In India itself voyages were granted from various ports, chiefly on the Coromandel coast, to numerous destinations. One ship sailed every year, for example, from Sao Thome to Malacca to buy spices and silk and another from the same port to southern Burma – Martaban and Tenasserim. In Malacca, the captain likewise sold voyages for ports on the Coromandel coast, and for Bengal, Burma and Siam, Sunda, Timor and Borneo. While these voyages and other viagens dos lugares appear to have been highly profitable for those fortunate enough or rich enough to obtain a licence, and sometimes moderately so for the crown, they did not lead to the Portuguese achieving greater control of the trade in the Bay of Bengal or in the Indonesian archipelago. Local coastal trade continued exactly as it had for centuries before the Portuguese arrived, and longer voyages along the principal trade routes of the area were still made by indigenous shipping, more often than not without the permission of the Portuguese authorities and sometimes even without their knowledge. For their part the Portuguese did not open up any new trade routes or introduce any new goods into the trading network of the area by means of which

they could have avoided the competition of indigenous merchants
altogether. They achieved nothing comparable to the galleon trade
between Manila and Acapulco, on which the economy of the Spanish
Philippines largely depended. The only port where the Portuguese
had an administration capable of collecting customs dues and the
authority to ensure they were paid was Malacca, and this was one
of the reasons why many indigenous merchants began to avoid
Malacca after the Portuguese conquest, unless they could be sure
of making a profit there in excess of what they would have to pay
in duties.

City Government

The essentially military character of Portuguese
government in the Estado da India and the failure, whether by
design or because of inadequate resources, of most of the
scattered Portuguese settlements in Asia to become substantial
colonies with large civilian populations made up of Portuguese,
mesticos and indigenous peoples all living under Portuguese
jurisdiction, meant that the Portuguese did little to develop
institutions of municipal government. This is in contrast to the
Spanish policy of conquista followed by reduccidn, through the
creation of ciudades and villas de espanoles, set up as provincial
capitals and social, religious and military centres from which to
disseminate Spanish influence and to consolidate Spanish
territorial control. The only exceptions were the five Asian
cities where the Portuguese exercised full sovereignty and
jurisdiction - Goa, Cochin, Colombo, Malacca and Macau. In these
cities alone was a municipal council or Senado da Câmara
established, and this again was in marked contrast to the Spanish
practice of instituting a cabildo or ayuntiamento in every
township in their empire.(40)

The Portuguese Câmaras were elective bodies and remained
on the whole resolutely independent of royal and viceregal
control. Their functions included the collection of taxes within
the municipality, the leasing of land and concessions, the upkeep
of bridges, roads, fountains and other civic amenities, the
granting of licenses to build, the certification of weights and
measures and the fixing of food prices. But they could also
exercise substantial political power and influence, since their
members were not crown officials appointed from outside but were
elected from among the leading citizens and were therefore
concerned to represent and defend the interests of the city. Most
of the members were unpaid: in Malacca at the time of its capture
by the Dutch in 1641 we are told that the treasurer, the
procurador and the secretary were paid salaries from municipal
funds, but the other aldermen and subordinate officials, such as
the almotaceis (market inspectors) and the juiz dos orfãos, were
not.(41)

The Câmaras were often the chief source of funds, not only for public works and to cover the cost of the numerous religious festivals celebrated by the Portuguese everywhere in their empire, but also for loans and levies to meet the expenses of the viceregal government in Goa and, on occasions, of the government in Lisbon. Thus, all the Câmaras in the Portuguese empire had to contribute to the dowry of Catherine of Braganca when she married Charles II of England and to the indemnity paid to the United Provinces at the conclusion of the Treaty of Breda in 1661.(42) The Câmara of Goa made frequent loans to help pay military and naval expenses, not only in India itself but also in other parts of the Estado da India: for example, it supplied most of the funds for the fleets sent to attack Johore in 1587 and for the relief of Malacca in 1606 and again in 1629.(43) The Câmara of Macau fitted out three junks to send to the aid of Malacca in 1640 when it was being besieged by the Dutch.(44)

The most powerful of the Câmaras in Portuguese Asia was the Senado da Câmara of Macau, which owed its exceptional degree of independence to the peculiar relationship that developed between the Portuguese settlement and the Chinese authorities, on whose complaisance and willingness to turn a blind eye to the irregularity of the Portuguese being there at all the existence of the colony depended.

The procurador of the city was a more important personage than the governor, whose authority was confined to the precincts of the fortaleza and the small body of men in the garrison there whom he commanded. He was also more important than the captain-major of the Japan voyage, for it was he who, as representative of the Câmara, negotiated with the provincial government of Kwangtung and petitioned the imperial court at Peking through the Jesuit missionaries there; and it was he who dealt with foreign rulers such as the Tokugawa shogun in Japan, the king of Ayuthya, the raja of Banjarmasin and the Dutch governor-general in Batavia. It was not until a royal decree of 9 January 1833 that the Senado da Câmara of Macau was deprived of its status as the principal authority in all dealings with the Chinese government and other Asian powers and was reduced to the position of a mere town council.(45)

The Macau Camâra was first established during the viceroyalty of Dom Francisco Mascarenhas (1581-84). Shortly after the Portuguese citizens of this rapidly growing city had agreed in June 1582 to swear allegiance to Philip II of Spain, who had recently ascended the Portuguese throne,

> [they] decided to arrange the form of local government in the same way as was practised in the cities of the kingdom and of the Estado da India; and in accordance with the statute they elected [ordinary] judges and aldermen, a procurador of the

city and a secretary of the Câmara. And they
entitled it the City of the Name of God in China,
which was the name by which it had been known up to
then.

Confirmation of this decision was obtained by a viceregal decree
signed at Goa on 10 April 1586. This decree granted to Macau the
same 'privileges, liberties, honours and pre-eminences' as those
possessed by the city of Evora in Portugal. The Câmara
subsequently tried to obtain the privileges of Oporto, but in
vain, and successive royal decrees of 1596, 1689 and 1709 only
ratified the original concession of 1586.(46)

At first the Câmara had only six members, all of whom
were prominent citizens. Elections were usually held every three
years, but occasionally annually. For these elections, the homens
bons of Macau would assemble in a junta geral and appoint six of
their number as electors. These six would then divide into two
groups of three and each group would send a list of candidates to
the viceroy. The viceroy in return would send back three lists of
six names selected from the names submitted to him, one for each
year of the triennium. Although some senators were reelected many
times by this system, their office was never allowed to become
hereditary and only rarely tenable for life. Two of the six acted
as judges (juizes ordinários), one for civil and one for criminal
jurisdiction, three as vereadores, and one as procurador. The
last was not only in charge of public works, chief of the
municipal treasury, superintendent of the customs and other
revenues, but was also, as we have seen, entrusted with the task
of dealing with the Chinese authorities in Kwangtung and paying
the annual dues into the imperial treasury. He was in addition
empowered by the Chinese government to deal with minor cases
arising in Macau between Chinese and Portuguese. From 1584 he was
given by the emperor all the titles and honours due to a mandarin
of the third class.(47)

From time to time extraordinary meetings of the Câmara
were held, to which were invited former senators, leading
merchants and shipowners, and some of the principal ecclesiastical
and civil authorities, such as the governor or the superior of the
Jesuits, Franciscans, Augustinians or Dominicans. Thus we find 62
people attending the meeting on New Years Day 1637 and 77 on 22
June 1643. The largest meetings were known as juntas gerais or
juntas do povo and were summoned for very special occasions, as
for example at the proclamation of the accession of Joao IV to the
Portuguese throne in May 1642 (over a year after the event took
place in Lisbon), when 276 people are recorded as having
attended.(48)

However, in spite of these occasional general meetings
attended by a wide cross-section of the citizens of Macau, the
Câmara remained a highly oligarchic and exclusive body and never

had any permanent artisan representation. In Goa the Câmara
counted among its members several procuradores dos mesteres or
attorneys for the guilds, who represented the artisans and
tradesmen of the city and were allowed full voting rights at
council meetings and were given the temporary status of gentlemen
to enable them to exercise these rights. In Macau on the other
hand the Câmara, like the council of Evora, on the charter (foral)
of which it was modelled, had no such representation. The only
members who had voting rights were the six elected senators.

The Portuguese in Timor

The Lesser Sunda Islands was the only area in the Estado
da India outside the Indian sub-continent where the Portuguese had
the time and the opportunity to extend their authority beyond the
core provided by the feitoria-fortaleza or the municipality to
cover a wider territory and embrace larger populations, made up of
Christians and non-Christians alike. It was the only area where
they could have attempted at an early date to create a form of
colonial administration that would not only have safeguarded their
commercial interests and protected their Christian missions but
might also have achieved for them a measure of control over the
territories that produced the goods in which they traded. The
Portuguese had first sailed to these remote islands in search of
the precious sandalwood that grew in abundance on the island of
Timor, and since 1561 the Dominicans had maintained a precarious
presence, at first on Solor, after 1613 at Larantaka on Flores,
and eventually also on Timor itself. (49)

Even in the Lesser Sunda Islands, however, the
establishment of Portuguese administration beyond the walls of the
fortalezas which the Dominicans and later the Portuguese military
authorities set up successively in Solor, Flores and Timor was
never seriously or systematically undertaken, chiefly because of
the extraordinary degree of antagonism to their presence that the
Portuguese encountered, especially in Timor. In the Lesser Sunda
Islands the extremely unsettled and confused situation made it
almost impossible for the Portuguese to assert military dominance
over the territories surrounding their fortalezas, let alone
introduce any civil administration or gain control over the
production of sandalwood, which had brought them there in the
first place. As we have already noted, the Portuguese possessions
in these islands were not even listed officially as parts of the
Estado da India until 1681. Throughout the sixteenth and
seventeenth centuries the Portuguese were continually harassed by
the internecine warfare that prevailed among the native rulers
(liurai) and their violent resentment of the Portuguese presence,
by the unruliness of the Topasses, the mestiço descendents of the
first Portuguese soldiers, seamen and traders from Malacca and

Macau to settle on Timor, whose leaders generally only gave nominal allegiance to the Portuguese crown and frequently entered into alliances with dissatisfied liurai against the Portuguese, and latterly by the unremitting hostility of the Dutch. Some captains were chased out almost as soon as they had disembarked, as for example Andre Coelho Vieira in 1697, while others never reached Timor at all, so that for long periods either there was no captain, or the Dominicans would appoint one on the spot, or one of the leading Topasses, usually a member of the Hornay or da Costa family, would arrogate the post to himself. As a result, although the authority of the captains was specifically declared to be separate from that of the Dominican vicar (vigario das cristandades de Solor), in practice the only effective control that the Portuguese had in these remote islands was exercised through the Dominicans.

It was only with the appointment in 1702 by the viceroy Antonio da Camara Coutinho of the secretary of the Estado da India, Antonio Coelho Guerreiro, as governor and captain-general of the islands of Solor and Timor that any concerted attempt was made to set up a regular military, civil and judicial establishment in the Lesser Sunda Islands on the model of other Portuguese possessions in Asia.

Coelho Guerreiro was given a free hand by the viceroy to impose order by whatever means he thought appropriate, not least in the judicial field. In the two sets of instructions (regimentos) confirming his appointment he was authorised to impose the death penalty without reference to any higher authority and was given 'full and ample power to do anything necessary for the better service of the king and the security of the islands and the increase of His Majesty's revenues, notwithstanding that it may not be expressly stated in this regimento'.(50) In practice, however, his authority remained extremely circumscribed. Coelho Guerreiro, having moved the seat of his government from Laruntuka in Flores to Lifau in present-day Oecusse in western Timor, was besieged there for two years by a group of Topasses under Domingos da Costa, until in 1704 he was forced to flee in disguise in an English ship commanded by Captain Alexander Hamilton, who has left us in his A New Account of the East Indies, published in Edinburgh in 1727, one of the best non-Portuguese accounts of Timor and of Portuguese rule in the island at that time. In most of the western part of Timor (Serviâo), the Dutch, though theoretically their rule was confined to their fortress at Kupang, had gained control by the middle of the eighteenth century, and had reduced Portuguese influence to the area in the immediate environs of Lifau. In the eastern part of the island (Belos) the Portuguese only exercised effective authority over those liurai who accepted their protection or suzerainty. In Flores, their power scarcely extended beyond Larantuka, and in Solor likewise Portuguese administration was confined to the small area within the walls of the fortaleza and to the small communities in the vicinity that had been converted to Christianity by the Dominican missionaries.

The governor's establishment at Lifau, and after 1769 at Dili, was of an even more markedly military character than was usual in these outposts of the Portuguese empire. The most important post in the military hierarchy was that of tenente-geral, which was usually held by a Timorese liurai or dato (nobleman). It did not qualify for any remuneration from the royal exchequer and the only real inducement to take it was the rank that it carried with it. Other military posts with appropriate ranks were also given to native chiefs or members of their families; at their head was the so-called emperor of Servião (the Sonaba'i), who was accorded the rank of brigadier. Coelho Guerreiro's policy of bestowing military ranks upon those liurai and dato who were more favourably disposed towards Portuguese rule marked the beginning of an attempt gradually to undermine the power of the liurai as independent rulers and bring them under Portuguese law and protection.

In the civil administration of Solor and Timor, the most important official after the governor was, as in Goa, the secretary. Both the secretary and the ouvidor, who combined his judicial functions with those of the auditor, juiz dos orfãos and provedor da fazenda dos defuntos e auzentes, were appointed by the governor.

Coelho Guerreiro's humiliating departure from Timor was followed by sixty years of warfare and disorder, with the Topasses and many of the native rulers, both in Belos and Servião, in a state of almost ceaseless rebellion and the Dutch gradually consolidating their power in the west of the island and reducing Lifau and its surroundings to the position of a small Portuguese enclave in Dutch territory. In 1769 the governor, António Teles de Meneses, decided to abandon Lifau and move his capital eastwards towards Dili. But this measure, while it amounted to an admission by the Portuguese that they had failed to gain mastery of western Timor and to subjugate the liurai of Servião, did not lead to any compensating assertion of Portuguese authority in the east. H. O. Forbes, who travelled in Timor in 1882, makes it clear in his account that, after almost two hundred years of Portuguese colonial rule, most of the liurai of Belos were still fully independent and indeed appeared to wield absolute power in their realms, though he noted among the liurai there were also various gradations of vassalage to each other. Forbes encountered no Portuguese officials, either civil or military, in the interior of the island and, wherever he went, it was the liurai and their appointed delegates who assumed responsibility for him and to whose jurisdiction he had to submit.(51)

It is clear from Forbes' account, as it is from other nineteenth century accounts of Timor, such as those of D. H. Kolf and Alfred Wallace, that Portuguese concepts of empire and colonial government, at least in Southeast Asia, had scarcely changed since the conquest of Malacca in 1511 and that they were still content to remain — or resigned to the necessity of remaining — in the small settlements they had established at certain points on the coasts and there to engage in trade and other mercantile pursuits, without trying to extend their administration into the interior, to bring native rulers under their sovereignty or to impose their law of the indigenous populations.(52) Nor had they attempted to gain control over the production of goods; in Timor sandalwood had been superseded since the middle of the nineteenth century by coffee as the principal export of the island, but the cultivation was confined to the hills around Dili, and in the rest of Portuguese Timor primitive forms of subsistence agriculture still prevailed, with many Timorese resorting to hunting and gathering in time of scarcity. Much the same situation seems to have obtained until late in the nineteenth century in Africa, where the Portuguese were nominally masters of very large colonial territories, far more extensive than east Timor, but where in practice the indigenous rulers still retained their independence virtually intact and the vast majority of the population had never been subjected to any sustained Portuguese influence.

As a result of the Berlin Conference of 1884-5, which drastically reduced the size of this inchoate Portuguese empire in Africa, the Portuguese at last made a concerted attempt by means of legislation to bring their remaining colonial possessions, including Timor, fully under their control. After the fall of Malacca to the Dutch in 1641, Portuguese Timor had passed under the direct authority of the viceregal government in Goa and it remained thus until 1844 when, with Macau, it was separated from the Estado da India to become an independent _governo_. This measure brought few advantages with it; indeed, Timor seems to have been even more neglected and worse administered under the authority of Macau than it had been under the viceregal government. In 1850, with the appointment of José Joaquim Lopes de Lima as governor-general, Timor was elevated to the status of an autonomous _governo_, no longer dependent on Macau. But this change brought no improvement in the administration of Timor, nor any alleviation of its poverty and backwardness, and in 1854 it again became a dependency of Macau. In the same year, an administrative structure was introduced into Timor similar to that imposed upon other Portuguese colonies, with a ruling council (Concelho do Governo), a treasury (Junta da Fazenda), and a municipal council (Câmara) in Dili. Most of the officials who served on these bodies, however, for lack of qualified civilians, were chosen from the governor's military staff.

By a decree of 1866, the post of governor of Timor was made subordinate to Macau and remained so till 1897, when the colony became an autonomous administrative unit (distrito autónomo) and was divided into eleven regions, each with its own

commander. These commanders did not, however, interfere with the
internal administration of the native kingdoms, nor, as Forbes'
account makes clear, did their authority supersede or even curtail
that of the liurai. On the contrary, they were obliged to seek
the consent of the independent liurai to any orders issued by the
governor of Dili, and it was not until 1912, with the suppression
of the last great uprising of the liurai, that a thorough-going
programme of pacification was instituted and Portuguese law and
administration introduced throughout the eastern half of the
island, based on a system of conselhos or circunscriçoes composed
of groups of villages (povoações). In 1904, a convention was
signed with the Dutch in which the division of the island between
the two colonial powers was agreed and the borders settled, and
any residual claims that the Portuguese still had to sovereignty
elsewhere in the Lesser Sunda Islands were abandoned. Portuguese
rule was henceforth confined to east Timor, the enclave of Oecusse
and the small island of Atauro.

After the establishment of the Estado Novo in Portugal in
1926 under the dictatorial rule of Salazar, the administration of
the Portuguese colonial empire was reorganised on more
authoritarian lines. By the Colonial Act of 1930, all Portugal's
overseas possessions, which under the monarchy had had the status
of "provinces" of the crown and in which the indigenous
populations had therefore enjoyed, at least theoretically, the
same rights and been subject to the same laws as Portuguese
subjects living in metropolitan Portugal, reverted to the status
of colonies, and the constitutional rights of the inhabitants, as
for example their right to vote or to have their children educated
by the state, became dependent upon whether they were classified
as assimilated (assimilados), and so deemed to be, by Portuguese
standards, civilised (civilisados). In Portuguese Timor in 1950
only 1.8 per cent of the adult population - Europeans, mestiços,
Chinese, other non-indigenous inhabitants (e.g. Goanese) and
indigenous civilisados were entitled to vote. The vast majority
of the inhabitants of Portuguese Timor therefore remained, as they
always had been, only nominally under Portuguese jurisdiction and
the writ of the Portuguese government only ran in those few areas
where there was a significant proportion of assimilados among the
population.(53)

Conclusion

With the exception of the few scattered territories in
India itself, in east Timor and Macau, where the Portuguese
remained in control for long enough to develop a form of colonial
government, comparable in the degree of authority it exercised
over the area in which it claimed hegemony and over the indigenous
population within its boundaries to the administrations set up by
the Spanish, Dutch, English and French in their Asian possessions,
the Estado da India remained throughout its existence very much as

it had been when it was first established. It scarcely developed any institutions either of central government or local administration, it produced no codified body of law, and it seldom achieved any clearly defined treaty relationships with the numerous states with which it competed for influence and for a share of the rich trade of the area. It remained, as it had been at the outset, an almost entirely unsystematic medley of jurisdictions and forms of administration, arising out of a series of independent decisions taken for the most part on the spot, not by professional administrators but by soldiers, merchants and missionaries, without reference to any central authority in Goa, still less in Lisbon, with few or no resources of men or money to support those decisions, and in response to a highly complex and constantly changing political and economic situation in an area spanning almost half the globe. The wonder is that under such adverse circumstances the Estado da India survived as long as it did.

Notes

1. Panduronga Pissurlencar (ed.), <u>Assentos do Concelho do Estado da India, 1618-1750</u>, 5 vols, (Bastora-Goa, 1953-57), IV, pp. 350-354. See also C.R.Boxer, <u>Portuguese India in the mid-seventeenth century</u> (Oxford University Press, 1980) p.19.

2. For an account of the medieval Portuguese <u>feitoria</u> and the early development of state capitalism by the Portuguese see Bailey W.Diffie and George D.Winius, <u>Foundations of the Portuguese Empire, 1415-1580</u> (University of Minnesota Press and Oxford University Press, 1977) pp.311-317. On the Casa de Guiné see Francisco Paulo Mendes da Luz, <u>O Conselho da India</u> (Lisbon, 1952) pp.29-57.

3. King to Almeida, March/April 1506, in Artur Basilio de Sa, <u>Documentação para a história das missões do padroado português do Oriente: Insulindia</u>, 5 vols, (Lisbon, 1954-58), I, pp.3-13. See also Regimento of Diogo Lopes de Sequeira, Almeirim, 13 February 1508, in Jeronimo Osorio, <u>De Rebus Emmanuelis Regis Lusitaniae Invictissimi Virtute et Auspicio Gestis</u>, 12 vols, (Lisbon, 1571), XII, p.417.

4. See L.F.F.R.Thomaz, 'Estrutura politica e administrativa do Estado da India no seculo XVI'. Paper presented to the second Seminario Internacional de História Indo-Portuguesa, Lisbon, October 1980, p.4.

5. See Robert R.Reed, <u>Colonial Manila: the context of Hispanic urbanism and process of morphogenesis</u> (University of California Press, 1978) pp.11-14.

6. Thomaz, 'Estrutura politica...', p.8.

7. See Niels Steensgaard, <u>The Asian trade revolution in the seventeenth century, the East India Companies and the decline of the caravan trade</u> (University of Chicago Press, 1973) pp.88-89; and C.R. de Silva, 'The <u>cartaz</u> system and monopoly trading in the Bay of Bengal: a study of the role of the Portuguese in Asian trade in the second half of the sixteenth century', paper presented to the IXth conference of the International Association of Historians of Asia, Manila, November 1983, pp.2-4.

8. Thomaz, 'Estrutura politica...' pp.9-10.

9. See John Villiers, '"De um caminho ganhar almas e fazenda": motives of Portuguese expansion in eastern Indonesia in the sixteenth century', <u>Terrae Incognitae</u>, 14, 1982, pp.29-30, and the sources cited there.

10. Villiers, 'De um caminho...', pp.29 and 30-31, and the sources cited there.

11. 'Livro das cidades e fortalezas que a coroa de Portugal tem nas partes da India e das capitanias e mais cargos que nelas ha e da importancia delles', in <u>Boletim da Biblioteca da Universidade de Coimbra</u>, XXI, 1953, p.108. Quoted in Artur Teodoro de Matos, <u>O Estado da India nos anos de 1581-1588: estrutura administrativa e econômica</u> (Ponta Delgada, 1982) p.18. This kind of undeclared extra-territoriality may be compared to that enjoyed by the European trading communities in the treaty ports of China in the nineteenth century. See Thomaz, 'Estrutura politica...', p.14.

12. See Hubert Jacobs SJ, <u>A Treatise on the Moluccas (c.1544)</u> (Rome, 1971) pp.201 and 350 and the sources cited there. This is probably the preliminary version of Antonio Galvão's lost <u>Historia das Molucas</u>.

13. On Viegas see John Villiers, 'The sandalwood trade and the first Portuguese settlements in the Lesser Sunda Islands'. Paper presented to the second Seminario International de Historia Indo-Portuguesa, Lisbon, October 1980, p.25.

14. Thomaz, 'Estrutura politica...', p.15.

15. On the Câmara of Macau see C.R.Boxer, <u>Portuguese society in the Tropics: the municipal councils of Goa, Macao, Bahia and Luanda 1510-1800</u> (University of Wisconsin Press, 1965) pp.42-71.

16. 'Livro das Cidades e Fortalezas...' 1582, p.24. Quoted in Matos, O Estado da India, pp.22-23.

17. Boxer, Portuguese India... p.9.

18. Ibid p.10.

19. Matos, O Estado da India, p.23.

20. On the career of Antonio Coelho Guerreiro see coronel Gonçalo Pimento de Castro, Timor. Subsidios para a sua história (Lisbon, 1944) pp.24-25; Humberto Leitao, Vinte e oito anos de história de Timor (1698 a 1725) (Lisbon, 1952) pp.13-87; C.R.Boxer, Fidalgos in the Far East, 1550-1770 (Oxford University Press, 1968) pp.183-188.

21. See Diffie and Winius, Foundations..., pp.325-27, and Matos, O Estado da India, pp.23-24.

22. See Alfredo Botelho de Sousa, Subsidios para a história militar maritima da India (1585-1669), 4 vols, (Lisbon, 1930), I, pp.22-24.

23. On the encomienda system in Castile and Spanish America see J.H.Elliot, Imperial Spain 1469-1716, Penguin Books (Harmondsworth, 1970) pp. 70-71; and in the Phillipines see Reed, Colonial Manila... p.81, n.21 and the sources there cited.

24. Almeida to king, Goa, 20 September 1508. Biblioteca Nacional de Lisboa. Fundo Geral 1461.

25. Tome Pires, Suma Oriental, trans. and ed. Armando Cortesão, 2 vols, Hakluyt Society, 2nd ser. 89 (London, 1944) p.204.

26. L.F.F.R.Thomaz, 'Malacca: the town and the soicety during the first century of Portuguese rule'. Paper presented to the VIIIth Conference of the International Association of Historians of Asia, Kuala Lumpur, 1980, pp.5-6. On the office of shahbandar in Indonesian port states see Purnadi Purbatijaraka, 'Shahbandars in the archipelago', Journal of Southeast Asian History, 2, pp.1-9.

27. For details of the population of Portuguese Malacca see Pedro Barreto de Resende, 'Descricoës das cidades e fortalezas da India Oriental...1635'. Biblioteca da Academia das Ciencias de Lisboa, MSS 267-68; 'Noticias a la India ano 1605', British Museum Add Mss 28461, fl 163; Manuel Godinho de Eredia, Declaraçam de Malaca (Brussels, 1882) pp.18-19.

28. See John Villiers, 'Portuguese Malacca and Spanish Manila: two concepts of empire'. Paper presented at the second British Institute in South-East Asia Historical Symposium, Manila, January 1981, pp.14-15.

29. 'Livro das cidades e fortalezas', p.35. Quoted in Matos, O Estado da India, p.18. One notable exception to the three year rule was Sancho de Vasconcellos, first captain of Ambon, who remained in office for almost twenty years from 1572 to 1591.

30. King to Matias de Albuquerque, 1 March 1594, in J.H.Cunha Rivara, Arquivo Portuguez Oriental, F.III, P.I doc. 140 (Nova Goa, 1861) p.423.

31. 'Livro do orcamento de rendimento de todas as fortalezas do Estado da India e das despezas ordinarias que fazem em cada hum anno, lancadas em seus titolos cada hum per sy', 1581, Arquivo Nacional do Torre do Tombo, F.A. no. 845, in Matos, O Estado da India, pp.181, 184.

32. See Hubert Jacobs SJ. 'The Portuguese town of Ambon, 1576-1605'. Paper presented to the second Seminario Internacional de Historia Indo-Portuguesa, Lisbon, October 1980, pp.5-6.

33. António de Brito to king, Ternate, 11 February 1523, in Sa, Documentacão..., I, p.153.

34. Matos, O Estado da India, p.20.

35. Diffie and Winius, Foundations..., p.320.

36. On these temporary feitorias in the Banda islands see John Villiers, 'Trade and society in the Banda Islands in the sixteenth century', Modern Asian Studies, 15, 4, 1981, pp.742-747.

37. In Southeast Asian waters most of the viagens dos lugares were made out of Macau. They included the Sunda voyage, which seems to have ceased at least by 1582, the Patani voyage, the Timor voyage for sandalwood, the voyage to Ayuthya, which was sometimes linked to a Japan voyage, the Banda voyage, the Moluccas voyage for cloves and the Ceylon voyage for cinnamon. A list of these voyages and a description of the part they played in the commercial organisation of the Estado da India are given in Matos, O Estado da India, pp.30-33. On the Japan voyage and its captaincy see C.R.Boxer, The great ship from Amacon. Annals of Macao and the old Japan trade, 1555-1640 (Lisbon, 1963). On the Moluccas voyage see L.F.F.R.Thomaz, 'Maluco e Malaca' in A viagem de Fernão de Magalhães e a questão dos Moluccas, Actas do II Coloquio Luso-Espanhol de História Ultramarina, (Lisbon, 1975). On the routes of these voyages and the commodities carried see L.F.F.R.Thomaz, 'Les portugais dans les mers de l'archipel au XVIe siecle', Archipel, 18, 1979, pp.105-125. See also Antonio Bocarro, 'Livro do Estado da India Oriental'. Biblioteca Nacional de Lisboa, cod. 11057, fl. 139v-140v. The viagens dos lugares were quite distinct and organised separately from the Carreira da India, which provided the commercial link between the Estado da India and Portugal via Goa and Cochin and, more rarely, Malacca.

38. 'Livro das cidades e fortalezas', p.129. Quoted in Matos, O Estado da India, p.31.

39. Ibid p.114. Quoted in Ibid, p.31.

40. On the institution of the cabildo in the Philippines and elsewhere in the Spanish empire see Luis Merino, OSA, El Cabildo Secular: aspectos fundacionales y administrativos (Manila, 1983) pp.1-20. An English edition of this work was published by the University of San Agustin, Iloilo, in 1980 under the title of The Cabildo Secular or municipal government of Manila. Social component, organisation, economics.

41. C.R.Boxer, The Portuguese Seaborne Empire, Pelican Books (Harmondsworth, 1973) p.281.

42. Boxer, Portuguese Society..., pp.79-80.

43. Ibid, p.19.

44. Ibid p.55.

45. Ibid p.49.

46. Ibid p.44.

47. Eusebio Arnais, 'The golden century of Macao', Philippine Historical Review, 1965, pp.47-49.

48. Ibid p.50.

49. On the Portuguese administration in Timor before 1702 see A.Faria de Morais, Solor e Timor (Lisbon, 1944); Humberto Leitao, Os Portugueses em Solor e Timor de 1515 a 1702 (Lisbon, 1948); Artur Teodoro de Matos, Timor Portugues 1515-1769: contribuiçao para a sua história (Lisbon, 1974); Boxer, Fidalgos in the Far East, pp.174-183; Villiers, 'Sandalwood trade...'.

50. These regimentos and other contemporary documents from the Arquivo Historico Ultramarino are transcribed by Matos in the Appendix of his Timor Portuguès. See especially doc. IV: 'Regimento para a matricula' [1702]; doc. VII: 'Regimento do Ouvidor, Auditor da Gente de Guerra, Juiz dos Orfaos, Provedor da Fazenda dos Defuntos e Ausentes das Ilhas de Solor e Timor e taxa dos salarios dos oficiais de justica das mesmas ilhas' [1702]. The best account of Guerreiro's governorship with much supporting documentation, is in Leitao, Vinte e oito anos, pp.13-87.

51. H.O.Forbes, 'On some of the tribes of the island of Timor', Journal of the Royal Anthropological Institute, 13, 1883, pp.402-430.

52. Alfred Russell Wallace, The Malay archipelago: the land of the

orangutan and the bird of paradise (London, 1880) pp.184-201; and
D.H.Kolff, Voyages...through the southern and little-known parts of
the Moluccan archipelago, and along the previously unknown southern
coast of New Guinea...1825-1826, ed. G.W.Earl (London, 1840) p.35

53. For one of the few impartial accounts of the later history of
Portuguese Timor up to the UDT coup of August 1975 and the
subsequent withdrawal of the Portuguese administration from Dili
see Jill Jolliffe, East Timor. Nationalism and Colonialism,
(University of Queensland Press, 1978) pp.26-28. Much of the
material for this section of the present paper is taken from this
source. See also Pimenta de Castro, Timor, especially pp.87-119
and 191-212.

Trade in the Indian Ocean and the Portuguese System of Cartazes

K.S. MATHEW

During the fifteenth century the Indian Ocean region was frequented by merchants of various nationalities, and commodities of diverse sorts were exchanged in its port towns. The picture presented was of a type of trade open to everyone irrespective of religion or nationality. This state of affairs prevailed until the end of the fifteenth century and then underwent substantial change in the early part of the sixteenth when a commercial revolution was effected and merchant capital began to exert great influence on the world of commerce and international politics. The Indian Ocean, frequently navigated by Arab sea-farers and Indian merchants, became the centre of the activities of the European traders supported directly or indirectly by their respective monarchies. This turn of events was inaugurated by the Portuguese navigators who opened up the direct sea-route to India and initiated a new system of control over the movements of the merchant shipping through the introduction of cartazes.

Areas like the East African coast, the ports of the Middle East such as Aden and Hormuz, the Gujerat, Konkan and Malabar coasts and the centres of Southeast Asian trade dominated by Malacca comprised the chief Indian Ocean regions where trade was conducted in the period prior to the sixteenth century. All these areas were interconnected through the exchange of commodities and the visits of merchants.

The trade with the ports in the areas between Egypt and China was chiefly dominated by Arab merchants at the time the Portuguese reached Indian shores. Mogadisho, Melinde, Mombasa, Zanzibar, Kilwa, Mozambique, Angoche and Sofala were some of the important centres of trade on the East African coast from where the Arab traders proceeded to the ports of the Indian subcontinent in search of commodities like cotton cloth, silk, other sorts of textiles and spices.(1) Great quantities of gold were taken from Monomotapa to Sofala and the Indian merchants supplied their commodities in exchange for gold. They made a great profit in this exchange. Hindu and Muslim merchants from Gujerat visited Mogadisho and the Somali coast with Indian textiles and collected gold, ivory and wax in exchange. They also took spices to Mogadisho to get ivory and gold which was in great demand in India.(2) Spices from Calicut were eagerly sought after in Sofala.

The Middle Eastern ports, especially Aden and Hormuz, served as the ports of entry for oriental goods that passed to the Mediterranean centres of trade and finally to various parts of western and northern Europe. The Arab merchants took copper, quicksilver, vermillion, saffron, rosewater, velvets, gold, silver and horses from these ports to India to exchange them for Indian commodities like spices and textiles.(3) The Italian merchants collected these oriental goods, especially spices, from Alexandria, Beirut, Cairo and Antioch, and distributed them to the various regions of Europe.(4) So in this international transaction, the ports of Aden, Jidda and Hormuz played an important role. Because of the trade in horses, Hormuz had very flourishing commercial relations with the ports of Gujerat, Konkan and Vijayanagar. Pepper, cinnamon, ginger and all sorts of drugs were taken to Hormuz and from there to Aden.(5)

The ports in the kingdom of Gujerat (Cambay), especially Broach, Diu, Surat and Tana, were connected with Hormuz and other ports of the Middle East and East African coast.(6) The Gujerati merchants were well known for their commercial activities and were compared to the Italian merchants by the writers of the early sixteenth century. Some of them conducted trade on their own, while a few were in the employment of other merchants. There were merchants from Cairo, Khurassan, Gilan, Aden and Hormuz who settled down in the various parts of the kingdom of Gujerat. Those from Cairo brought gold, silver, quicksilver, vermillion, copper, rosewater, camlets, scarlet-in-grain, coloured woollen cloth and glass beads which they got from Italy, Greece and Damascus to Aden and from there these items along with madder, raisins, opium, rosewater, gold and silver were transported to the various ports of the kingdom of Gujerat. These foreign merchants purchased cloves, nutmeg, mace, sandalwood, brazilwood, silks, seed pearls, musk, porcelain, rice, wheat, soap, indigo, oils, cornelians, coarse pottery and all kinds of cloth in the port towns of Gujerat in exchange for the commodities they brought.(7)

Ports of the Konkan coast also had a very active trade in the period prior to the arrival of the Portuguese. Dabhol, Danda, Chaul and Goa were some of the important centres of trade. The port of Dabhol was always crowded with horses coming from Hormuz and Aden. Calicos and beatilhas produced in Dabhol and Chaul were in great demand in Hormuz and Aden and trade in Chaul made great strides under Ahmad Nizam Shah and his successors.(8) Horses from Persia and Arabia were imported into Goa in great numbers till it came under the sway of the Portuguese. Merchants of all

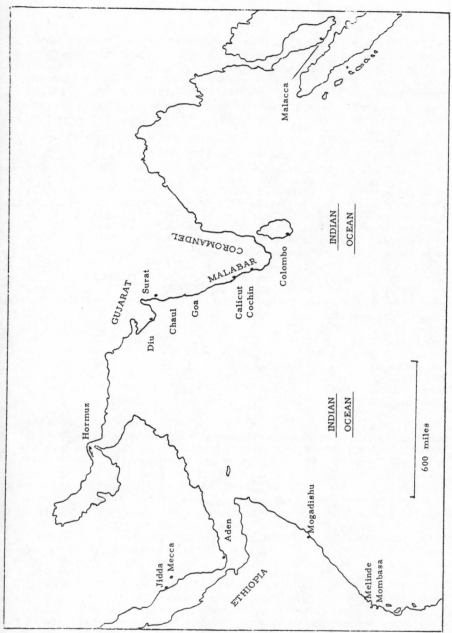

Map 2 The Indian Ocean

nationalities were found busying themselves in trade in this port.
Horses were re-exported from Goa to Vijayanagar and other parts of
the Deccan. The merchants from Hormuz collected rice, sugar,
iron, pepper, ginger and other spices of different sorts from the
port-towns of the Konkan coast. Similarly Honawar, Bhatkal,
Basrur (Bacalor), Barkur (Bacanor) and Manglore, all south of Goa,
were also frequented by the merchants from Hormuz, Mecca, Gujerat
and Malabar.(9)

On account of the availability of pepper, and various
sorts of spices, the ports on the Malabar coast were havens for
merchants from all over the world of commerce, and among the
several ports of this region, Calicut occupied the most important
position in international trade.(10) Muslim merchants from Mecca,
Aden, Tenasseri, Pegu, Ceylon, Turkey, Persia, Ethiopia and Egypt
were found in large numbers in Calicut prior to the arrival of the
Portuguese. Even merchants from Tunis, speaking Castilian, were
present at Calicut when Vasco da Gama reached there in 1498.(11)
In fact, until the first half of the fifteenth century Chinese
merchants frequented the port of Calicut and maintained there a
factory of their own which was called Cinakotta.(12) The Gujerati
merchants were the prominent ones among the Indians and they had
their settlements in Cannanore, Calicut and Cochin. Copper,
quicksilver, vermillion, coral, saffron, carpets, porcelain, tin,
coloured velvets, gold, silver, raisins, opium, madder, horses and
textiles were brought to the ports on the Malabar coast for the
purchase of pepper, ginger, cinnamon, cardamons, myrabolans,
tamarind, canafistula, amber, rhubarb, aloes-wood, cloves nutmeg,
mace, sandalwood, brazilwood, betel, coconut, jaggery and
arecanuts.(13)

The trading centres of Southeast Asia, especially
Malacca, were flooded with merchants from various parts of the
world. The trade of this area was chiefly in the hands of the
Arab Muslim merchants and others of Southwest Arabia, Oman, Persia
and also of Jews. The merchants of Calicut traded with Malacca in
great number. Most of the merchants, including those from the
Indian subcontinent, exchanged Indian commodities, chiefly
textiles, for cloves from the Moluccas, nutmegs and mace from
Banda, sandalwood from Timor, camphor from Borneo, gold and silver
from Sumatra and Liu Kiu and other aromatic goods from China, Java
and Siam. All the various sorts of commodities from the Southeast
Asian region were brought to Malacca which thus became the
greatest emporium of the East.(14) Among the Indian merchants,
the Cettis of the Coromandel coast and the Gujeratis occupied an
important position in Malacca. There were more than a thousand
Gujerati merchants settled in Malacca in addition to the four to
five thousand merchants who frequented Malacca every year for the
sake of trade. The Gujerati merchants in Malacca had their own
shahbandar there.(15)

Thus trade in the Indian Ocean was totally free and no one tried to impose any restrictions on the movement of merchants and merchandise. Traders from one region of the Indian Ocean were found trading in another and there does not appear to have been any merchandise under any sort of monopoly. No class or group was favoured or discriminated against. It was this sort of free trade, dominated chiefly by the muslim merchants, that the Portuguese wanted to control and monopolise for themselves. Their aspirations to appropriate trade in the Indian Ocean were based on certain assumptions which did not stand the test of actual encounter with the existing systems in the East.

In the first place, they expected that they could enter into close alliance with the supposed christian king of the East and exploit the communality of faith to extract the necessary commodities and to establish commercial superiority. As is clearly testified by Vasco da Gama on his arrival at Calicut, they were looking for 'Christians and Spices'. It was hoped that the papal bulls, beginning with <u>Romanus Pontifex</u>, which they had obtained in the fifteenth century would be of value to them in their efforts. However, to their great surprise, the rulers on the west coast of India were not Christians at all. Thus they were baffled in their attempts to establish an alliance with christian kings.

The Portuguese envisaged a political vacuum in the Indian Ocean region and in their haste to establish supremacy and to control the movements of foreign ships Dom Manuel, the king of Portugal, added one more epithet to his grandiloquent title and styled himself as <u>Senhor da Navegaçăo, Conquista e Commercio da Ethiopia, Arabia, Persia e India</u> in 1501.(16) After Pedro Alvares Cabral met with a serious rebuff from the Samorin of Calicut, from whom the Portuguese demanded exclusive rights to trade with Calicut, Vasco da Gama reached the Malabar coast in 1502 with a fleet of 15 well-equipped ships ready to fight against his rivals in this region. As the rulers of Cannanore, Cochin and Quilon were, for various reasons, sympathetic towards the Portuguese, Vasco da Gama decided to spare the ships belonging to those three kingdoms. The Portuguese admiral placed the demand before the Samorin that he should expel all the muslim merchants, both Indian and foreign, from Calicut and not a single Muslim should be permitted to have any relations with any port in his kingdom. There were about five thousand muslim families residing in Calicut itself at that time. The Samorin stated in unequivocal terms that his port and kingdom would remain open to everyone and thus he turned a deaf ear to the Portuguese request. So fierce naval battles were fought in this region and the Portuguese, with a view to sparing the vessels of the above-mentioned kingdoms, introduced an expedient under which those ships that were not to be attacked were required to carry a certificate duly signed by the Portuguese authorities, namely the royal factor. This certificate was called a <u>cartaz</u> and it was first issued in 1502.(17)

Later, the Portuguese officials were detailed to guard the coastal regions with a view to preventing other ships from conducting trade with any part of India and they were asked to capture and confiscate all the ships that were not equipped with cartazes.(18) Merchants and rulers interested in sending their commodities to the various places like Hormuz, or coming to the different ports of India were constrained to take cartazes from the Portuguese as they found it necessary, and this became a regular practice.(19) The captain of the respective fortress or the official of the factory issued the cartazes.(20) Lopo Soares, the governor of Portuguese India in 1518, issued orders that there should be a book in which all the cartazes issued from time to time could be registered and this book was to be shown to him whenever he desired to consult it. The cartazes were to be made out by the writers of the factory who were entitled to have a share in the perquisites, but these cartazes were to be signed by the authorities of the factory or fortress. At times an amount of five pardãos for each cartaz was charged to the parties concerned.(21)

The merchants of Cochin, like Cherina Marakkar, used to purchase cartazes from the factory at Cochin to send their merchandise to Hormuz. Malik Gopi, the great merchant governor of Surat, collected cartazes for his ships to be sent to Malacca and other regions of Southeast Asia. In return for defending the cause of the Portuguese at the court of Champaner, Malik Gopi insisted that the Portuguese should issue cartazes for the Gujerati ships to trade with Malacca and the surrounding areas. Later Amir Gopi, his son otherwise called Mircopi, collected twenty cartazes at a time from the Portuguese for his ships to be sent to Dabhol around 1533.(22) Despite his inveterate enmity towards the Portuguese, Khwajar Safar, the merchant governor of Surat in the kingdom of Gujerat purchased cartazes from the captains of Bassein and Diu for his ships to be sent to Suez and Jidda.(23) Khwaja Schams-ud-din Giloni, the administrator of Asad Khan, the governor of Belgaum in the kingdom of Bijapur, had trade with Malacca, Jidda, Ormuz, Diu and the Moluccas, and he sent even pepper, an item of royal monopoly under the Portuguese, to the Middle East in the ships equipped with cartazes issued by the Portuguese.(24) Abu Bakar Ali, the uncle of Adiraja (Ali Raja?) of Cannanore on the Malabar coast, got cartazes from the Portuguese to send his ships with commodities to various parts of India and abroad and he himself instructed his people to continue this practice. So the merchants of Cannanore continued this religiously and in 1546 the muslim merchants sending their ships to Mecca were found carrying the cartazes from the Portuguese.(25) The number of merchants purchasing cartazes went on increasing as the Portuguese sphere of influence and might spread far and wide. Both Indian and foreign traders collected cartazes from the Portuguese officials in Cochin, Cannanore, Goa, Chaul, Bassein, Daman and Diu. This practice continued to be in vogue even in the second half of the eighteenth century and there were instances of cartazes being issued to various merchants of Mangalore, Barcelor, Bedrur, Bidanur, Condapur, Honawar, Karwar, Goa, Rajpaur, Surat, Broach, Goga, Kutch and Kutch Mandovi for their ships to Bassora, Hormuz, Aden, Bengal and Congo.(26)   Even the Armenian merchants collected cartazes from the Portuguese for their vessels.(27)

It was not only the fate of the merchants to be constrained to purchase cartazes from the Portuguese, but rulers also, from local chieftains up to the great Emperor of the Mughals, were bound to do so if they wanted their ships to be safe and secure in the Indian Ocean.   The king of Cannanore used to collect cartazes for more than ten ships a year and sent them laden with commodities to Cambay and Hormuz.   He was at times permitted to import horses to the Malabar coast.(28)   The ruler of Tanur on the Malabar coast, who was friendly with the Portuguese from the first decade of the sixteenth century, obtained cartazes from them for his ships.(29)   The Samorin of Calicut too agreed to collect cartazes from them for his ships and it was also stipulated that all those vessels from Hormuz, Gujerat, Malacca, Sumatra, Pegu, Tenasserim, Bengal, Coromandel, Ceylon, Jafnapatam and Chaul coming to Calicut should carry the Portuguese cartazes.   The Portuguese, while concluding a treaty with Bahadur Shah, the sultan of Gujerat, concerning the surrender of Bassein, agreed to issue cartazes to all the ships of the sultan and his men which left for any part of the world.(30)   He was expected to pay a nominal amount for the passes.   The Nizam Shah of Ahmednagar, in the light of the terms of the treaty signed on 22 April 1539, collected cartazes from the Portuguese for his ships, and Hussain Shah (1553-65) obtained cartazes from them in 1561 for the ships with a view to importing horses.(31)

The Samorin of Calicut got cartazes from the Portuguese during the time of Afonso de Noronha, the viceroy (1550-54), for sending his ships.   The rulers of Tanur and Chale on the Malabar coast obtained cartazes in 1550 from them to send their ships to Mecca.   The Adil Shah of Bijapur and Nizam Shah of Ahmednagar sent three ships to the Straits of Mecca in 1563 with the cartazes issued by the Portuguese.(32)   The Samorin in fact obtained permission around 1568 from them to send two ships every year to Mecca with 300 bhars of pepper.(33)   Around 1598 he got cartazes for five ships every year to send to the Middle East.(34)   From the time of Akbar the Great, each of the the Mughal emperors collected a cartaz free of charge every year from the Portuguese for the ship to be sent to Mecca.   The king of Cochin, even in the first half of the seventeenth century, sent his ships with the cartazes issued by the Portuguese.   The Adil Shah of Bijapur obtained permission from them for six ships going to Mecca, Hormuz and others ports in 1613.   According to the practice that came to be in use, the Emperor Janhangir collected a free cartaz every year from them to send his ship to Mecca.   Similarly Nizam Shah of

Ahmednagar got <u>cartazes</u> from them for his ships to be sent to various ports.(35)

Thus both the merchants and the rulers of the region were bound to purchase <u>cartazes</u> for the security of their ships and for the right to import or export certain commodities which were declared as monopoly items by the Portuguese. This system introduced by the Portuguese was rather irksome to everyone. Though the payment for the <u>cartazes</u> was negligible, it involved a lot of difficulty for those who had to obtain them. In the case of the merchants of Gujerat, the amount to be paid for a <u>cartaz</u> was fixed at a <u>tanga</u> each, but all the ships were obliged to visit a particular port and collect the <u>cartazes</u> from there. In addition to this, they were enjoined to visit a definite port indicated by the Portuguese and pay the taxes for the commodities carried.(36)

A <u>cartaz</u> thus issued contained reference to the circumstance in which it was given. The name and the tonnage of the ship, the age and name of the its captain, the port of embarkation as well as disembarkation, and the approximate date of departure were also indicated in the <u>cartaz</u>. Mention was made of the arms and ammunition carried in the ship and the items that were prohibited to be transported were also declared. Lastly the names of the writers and of the issuing authority were given along with the date of issue. The Portuguese, in the treaties of peace and friendship with the various rulers in the East, insisted on their obligation to comply with the regulations regarding the <u>cartazes</u> and the rulers accepted it under the conditions stipulated in the treaties.

It is of interest to glance at the theory developed by the Portuguese writers to justify this presumptuous step taken by the Portuguese discoverers to oblige the merchants and rulers of the Orient to purchase <u>cartazes</u>. The ideas that were current in Portugal during the sixteenth century were expressed by Joao de Barros who wrote in 1552 arguing that the popes were the supreme and universal authorities able to distribute among the faithful those lands which were not under christian control. They had permitted the kings of Portugal to conquer and appropriate the areas they had discovered or would discover. Consequently, on the strength of the three juridical titles (discovery, occupation and conquest) the Portuguese king could claim absolute power over the Indian Ocean region. Through the efforts of Vasco da Gama and Pedro Alvares Cabral, the king of Portugal discovered the navigation of hitherto unknown seas to reach the Orient from Portugal. After the discovery he took possession of the maritime route. He discovered that the lands were inhabited by idolaters and Muslims, and took these areas from them as they were deemed to be unjust possessors who denied the glory due to the Creator and Redeemer. He discovered that the trade in spices was in the hand of the infidels and, as he was the lord of the sea route, it was befitting that he should be lord of the commerce too. As far as navigation was concerned, the Portuguese were quite powerful in the Indian Ocean and so they were in reality the lords thereof. Hence the Hindus and Muslims were rightfully compelled to purchase cartazes.

Even though the seas were held to be common and were open to all, this was valid, Barros asserted, only in Europe among Christians and not at all among those who did not believe in the Roman church of Jesus Christ. Thus he propounded the idea of the mare clausum and the exclusive right of the Portuguese to trade with the Indian Ocean region.(37) His arguments, put forward in the first half of the sixteenth century to defend the Portuguese supremacy over the Indian Ocean, present the quintessence of the thought current in Europe and especially in Portugal.

However, not all the merchants and rulers abided by the rules and regulations issued by the Portuguese. The Portuguese system insisted on the delivery of commmodities at the price fixed at the dawn of the sixteenth century.(38) The Samorin of Calicut, displeased with the price offered by the Portuguese, sent forty-two of his vessels loaded with pepper to Diu in 1523.(39) Adiraja of Cannanore had a very important trade in pepper with the Laccadives around 1568 and dispatched his ships in contravention of the Portuguese restrictions once war had broken out between himself and the Portuguese in 1559.(40)

The attitude of some at least of the private Indian merchants was the same. Despite the risk of being captured by the Portuguese, they sent their ships laden with commodities to various places where they could obtain a better price. Regardless of the stringent measures adopted by the Portuguese towards such attempts, ships loaded with spices appeared in the Red Sea around 1513. About this time twelve or thirteen ships carrying pepper and other merchandise left the Malabar coast for Mecca and Aden. Also in the same year almost the same number of vessels were found ready to proceed to the same destination. Mohammed Macary, the chief merchant of Calicut, sent spices loaded in three vessels from Calicut to Cairo in 1513. Small vessels carried pepper to Chaul and Diu from the Malabar coast in 1520, unmindful of the Portuguese system of cartazes. The merchants from Jidda came to Calicut to purchase pepper even though there were two fortresses in its vicinity and the local merchants supplied the required quantity of pepper. This risk was taken by them because the gains were quite attractive and worth the trouble, as they themselves confessed.(41)

Large quantities of pepper were taken to the Coromandel coast through the interior parts of South India on bullocks and as headloads. Vilinjam, Aryankavu and Puthra were some of the places through which this "unauthorised" traffic was carried on.(42) Around 1547, it was reported that the local merchants sent several

ships loaded with pepper to Mecca and they never cared to collect
the cartazes from the Portuguese officials.(43) The practice of
the local merchants breaking the Portuguese monopoly and sending
ships to various ports in India and abroad without cartazes
continued also in the second half of the sixteenth century. It
was estimated that out of the 60,000 quintals of pepper produced
annually in the area between Calicut and Cape Comorin, only 15,000
were delivered to the Portuguese factories and the rest, that is
three-fourths, was taken "illegally" to other parts.(44) Several
merchants who were under the Mughals but were settled in Surat,
Mangrol and Kutch, conducted similar trade with the protection
given by the English and other western European powers in the
seventeenth century.(45) This bears out the fact that a
considerable trade was being conducted in the Indian Ocean region
by the merchants and rulers despite the monopolist and prohibitory
measures adopted by the Portuguese. Only one-fourth of the total
produce of pepper reached the Portuguese factories in India in
spite of the desperate attempts made by them. In other words, the
Portuguese system of cartazes did not bear the required fruit.

Side by side with the practical violation of the
Portuguese supremacy enforced through the system of cartazes,
theoretical treatises, challenging Portuguese rights, appeared in
various parts of the world. Presumably the wave of protestant
revolution that was rampant in the Low Countries and the
inveterate enmity of the Netherlanders towards the Spanish throne,
prompted them to call the papal bulls in question and flout the
Portuguese supremacy. This was aggravated by the fact that the
Spanish king, who since 1580 was also the king of Portugal,
prohibited the sale of the spices to the protestants. Hugo
Grotius, with a view to justifying the capture of the Portuguese
galleon, Santa Caterina, published in 1608 his Mare Liberum
attacking the monopolist attitude of the Portuguese, and defending
the rights of the Vereenigde Oost-Indische Compagnie.

The English, going a step further than the merchant
adventurers of the Levant Company, also established the English
East India Company and acquired footholds in the port towns of
India. The English mind too was not ready to accept the arguments
put forward by the Portuguese and the Dutch as a final verdict on
the subject and so jeopardise their commercial interests. William
Welwood published the booklet An Abridgement of the all the
Sea-Lawes in 1613 providing the theoretical background for the
British claims to the dominion of the sea. John Selden defended
the right of the British crown to appropriate the sea as well as
the land and refuted the ideas expressed in Mare Liberum. His
tract entitled Mare Clausum was written in 1617 or 1618 and in it
he attacked the Dutch position. In 1619 Welwood wrote another
book entitled De Dominio Maris Juribusque ad Dominium praecique
spectantibus Assertio brevis ac methodica. This too argued
against the opinion of Grotius. Seraphim de Freitas, a Portuguese
writer and professor at the university of Valladolid, asserted and

reaffirmed the rights of the Portuguese and published a number of arguments refuting those of Grotius and other theorists. This book entitled De Justo Imperio Lusitanorum Asiatico was published in 1625. Thus both the Portuguese and the Dutch claims for dominion of the Indian Ocean and the adjacent areas were challenged by interested parties who vied with each other for the free trade in the Indian Ocean region. By the second half of the seventeenth century, the Portuguese were confined to the colonies of Goa, Daman and Diu giving way to other European powers.

The picture that emerges from the discussion of trade in the Indian Ocean region prior to the arrival of the Portuguese is one of free trade wherein merchants and rulers from various parts of the countries bordering the Indian Ocean could take part without fear or favour of anybody. Traders from Africa, Hormuz and so on were found in the far distant port of Malacca where the Gujaratis too had established their merchant settlements on a strong footing, even having their own shahbandar. These merchants were also found exchanging commodities on the eastern coast of Africa, and bringing gold and ivory to India. Similarly the people of Hormuz and Aden had trade with the various Southeast Asian countries. The merchants of Gujarat went to the ports of the Middle East to collect certain commodities available there and added a few more from Gujarat to the list of merchandise and took them to the Konkan coast, the Malabar coast and the regions of Southeast Asia. The Samorin of Calicut welcomed merchants from all over the world, extended them special assistance and gave them one or two experienced traders like the Gujaratis to instruct them in the local customs and manners. However, we come across no treaties between kings and merchants as far as the Indian Ocean region was concerned. No instance of monopoly claimed by any particular group of merchants or rulers is seen in the period before the sixteenth century. There were no commodities declared as prohibited and no monopolies.

The sixteenth century and the early part of the seventeenth witnessed hectic activity, both in the field of theory and practice, on the part of the Portuguese to claim supremacy over the Indian Ocean regions. The establishment of fortresses in the region from East Africa to Malacca shows their practical efforts in this line. Insistence on the necessity for purchasing cartazes and the confiscation of ships which did not carry them, point to the same thing. The treaties concluded with the various rulers of India made it clear that the rulers should abide by the obligation to take cartazes and this was extended also to all the merchants. A number of them followed this, though there were a lot of cases where no attention was paid. The theorists hailing from the various maritime nations propounded ideas buttressing their own claims. As the European countries abandoned the framework of their medieval ideas, the papal authority was no longer respected, though the Portuguese tried to make much out of it for their own interest. As a result the rivalries in the

Indian Ocean led to frequent naval battles and finally the Portuguese had to give way to the other powers.

It cannot be substantiated that the system of cartazes introduced by the Portuguese had an all-permeating effect. Several merchants and rulers disregarded it totally, and in the seventeenth century they used to obtain cartazes from all the European powers for one and the same ship. This speaks for the ineffectiveness of the Portuguese cartaz system and betrays the weakness of Portuguese power in the Indian Ocean. As some of the ships of the Portuguese went on patrolling the Indian Ocean region, the merchants interested in higher prices began to use alternative routes crossing the mountain ranges to reach the eastern coast rather than going along the western coast. This paved the way for the development of a number of new routes and trading centres.

Notes

1. Codex Fronteira No.M. 4 fols. 192-286; Luciano Ribeiro, 'Uma Geografia Quinhentista' in Studia, 7, 1961, pp.181-189.

2. Ibid pp.183, 187, 189.

3. Fernão Lopes de Castanheda, História do Descobrimento e Conquista da India pelos Portugueses, livro 1, (Coimbra, 1924) p.7; Ibid pp.381-3.

4. Gaspar Correa, Lendas da India, tomo 1, (Coimbra, 1922) p.9.

5. Tomé Pires, The Suma Oriental of Tomé Pires, Hakluyt Society, reprinted 1967, pp.20-1.

6. K.S.Mathew, 'Trade and Trading Centres in the Early Sixteenth Century Gujarat' in V.K.Chavda & K.S.Mathew eds. Studies in Trade and Urbanisation in Western India (Baroda, 1984) pp.15 ff.

7. Tomé Pires, op. cit. pp.41-43.

8. K.S.Mathew, 'The Sea-borne Trade of the Nizam Shahi Kingdom of Ahmednagar and the maritime supremacy of the Portuguese' (unpublished paper); Raymundo António de Bulhão Pato, ed. Cartas de Affonso de Albuquerque, tomo 1, (Lisbon, 1884) p.343; Castanheda, op. cit., livro 3, p.289.

9. Duarte Barbosa, The Book of Duarte Barbosa, vol 1, Hakluyt Society, reprinted 1967, p.178; Ibid pp.185-195; Tomé Pires, op. cit. pp.60-62.

10. K.S.Mathew, Portuguese Trade with India in the Sixteenth Century (New Delhi, 1983) pp.10-28.

11. Montalbodo, Paesi nouvamente retrovati & Novo Mondo da Alberico Vesputio Florentino Intitulato, reprint, (Princeton, 1916) p.31; Damião Peres ed., Diario da Viagem de Vasco da Gama (Porto, 1945), vol 1, p.59; Correa, op. cit., vol 1, pp.75-9.

12. Garcia da Orta, Coloquios dos simples e drogas da India (Lisbon, 1891), vol I, p.205; W.W.Rockhill, 'Notes on the relations and trade of China with the Eastern Archipelago and the coast of the Indian Ocean during the fourteenth century', Tong Pao, vol xv, Leiden, 1914 (for the detailed study of the Chinese relations).

13. Barbosa, op. cit., vol II, p.73; Montalbodo, op. cit. pp.94, 161; Barbosa, op.cit., vol II, p.77; Tomé Pires, op. cit., pp.43, 78; Castanheda, op. cit., livro II, pp.381-3.

14. Barros, op. cit., decada I, part 2, pp.174ff; Tomé Pires, op. cit., pp.97-130; Barbosa, op. cit., vol II, pp.169-208.

15. Tomé Pires, op. cit. p.45; Castanheda, op. cit., livro III, p.135.

16. "Lord of the Navigation, Conquest and Commerce of Ethiopia, Arabia, Persia and India". See Barros, op. cit., decada I, part 2, pp.11, 19.

17. Correa, op. cit., tomo 1, p.298.

18. Barros, op. cit., decada I, part 2, p.21; decada II, part 1, p.181.

19. Marino Sanuto, I Diarii di Marino Sanuto, tomo iv, (Venice, 1881) col. 367.

20. J.H.Cunha Rivara, Archivo Portuguese Oriental, fasciculo V, part I, (Goa, 1865) pp.30-1.

21. Historical Archives of Goa (hereafter HAG) Codex no. 3027
    'Provisões, Alvaras e Regimentos', part I, fol. 93; Ibid, Codex
    3027, fol 21v.

22. Bulhão Pato, op. cit., tomo I (Lisbon, 1881) p.49; Correa, op.
    cit., tomo II, p.215; Ibid p.354; Ibid tomo III, pp.543-4.

23. K.S.Mathew, 'Khwaja Safar, the merchant governor of Surat and the
    Indo-Portuguese trade in the early sixteenth century', Proceedings
    of the Indian History Congress (Kurukshetra, 1982) p.237.

24. Archivo Nacional da Torre de Tombo (hereafter ANTT), Corpo
    Chronologico (hereafter CC), 1-79-134; ANTT, Collecção de S.
    Lourenco, III, fols 134, 185.

25. Armando Cortesão e Luis de Albuquerque eds., Obras Completas de
    D.João de Castro, vol II, (Coimbra, 1976) pp. 110-11; Ibid p.447.

26. HAG Codex no 1363, fol 48; codex no 1063, fols 31, 34v; 35, 41v;
    42; codex no 1363, fols 48v-49; 50, 47, 51, 49, 53v-54; codex no
    1063, fols 37v; 36; codex no 1363, fols 139, 90, 92v; codex no
    1063, fols 27, 27v; 28, 30, 37; 39; codex no 1363, fols 45v-46, 52,
    58, 74v-75; codex no 1083, fols 28v, 29r; codex no 1363, fols
    91v-92, 95; 96; 197.

27. HAG Codex 1063, fols 38v-39, 45; codex 1363, fols, 47v-48.

28. ANTT Nucleo Antigo, no 891.

29. Bulhão Pato, op. cit., tomo I, p.321.

30. Julio Firmino Judice Biker, Collecção de Tratados e Concertos de
    Pazes que o Estado da India Portugueza fez com os Reis e
    Senhores..., tomo I, (Lisbon, 1881) pp.21-23; Ibid p.63.

31. Simão Botelho, 'Tombo do Estado da India' in Rodrigo José de Lima
    Felner ed., Subsidios para História da India Portugueza (Lisbon,
    1868) pp.115-117; ANTT. CC. 1-105-75.

32. ANTT. CC. 1-105-75; ANTT.CC. 1-83-90; ANTT.CC. 1-107-38.

33. Archivum Romanum Societatis Jesu (hereafter ARSJ), Codex Goa 38,
    fols 352-375.

34. Diogo do Couto, op. cit., decada XII, p.239.

35. HAG Codex 1043, fol 50; Ibid fol 63; Livros dos Monçoẽs, tomo VI-A,
    fol 81; Ibid fols 67-71; Ibid fol 50; Ibid fols 59-62.

36. Biker, op. cit., pp. 63, 69.

37. Barros, op. cit., decada I, part II, pp. 14-19; K.S.Mathew, 'Portuguese trade with India and the theory of royal monopoly in the sixteenth century', Proceedings of the Indian History Congress (Waltaire, 1979) pp.389-396.

38. Thomé Lopes, 'Navegação as Indias Orientais', in Collecção da Noticias para a História e Geografia das Nações Ultramarinas que vivem nos Dominios Portugueses ou lhes são vizinhos, tom II, nos I & 2, (Lisbon, 1812) p.194; Barros, op. cit., decada 1, part II, p.18.

39. Sanuto, op. cit., vol XXXVI, (Venice, 1893) col 514.

40. ARSJ. Goa-38, fol 370.

41. Bulhão Pato, op. cit., tomo I, p.180; Ibid, tomo III, p.50; Ibid, tomo IV, p.179; Ibid, tomo VII, p.174; Ibid, tomo I, p.126.

42. Ibid, tomo VII, p.175.

43. Cortesão e Albuquerque, op. cit. p.447.

44. Josef Wicki ed., 'Duas Relações sobre a Situação da India Portuguesa nos anos 1568 e 1569', Studia, 8, 1961, p.155.

45. A.B.de Braganza Pereira, Arquivo Portugues Oriental (Bastora, 1937), tomo IV, vol II, part 1, p.114.

Goa in the Seventeenth Century

ANTHONY DISNEY

In recent years there has been some rekindling of
interest in Goa's history, accompanied by a diversity of views on
how it may best be approached and written. Should Goa be
portrayed as primarily a commercial seaport and therefore be
studied mainly within the context of Indian Ocean trade? Or
should greater recognition be given to the fact that most Goans
lived by subsistence agriculture, and more stress therefore be
placed on the life of the villages and the routines of the
countryside? On another plane, is it more appropriate to regard
Goa as falling firmly within the Portuguese political, economic
and cultural orbits from the early sixteenth to the mid twentieth
centuries, or should she, on the contrary, be presented as
indissolubly part of the mainland, overwhelmingly Indian in
character and essence, throughout this period? And if Portuguese
rule was never more than superficial and Goa derived little of her
distinctiveness from Portuguese associations, what, if anything,
gives her a particular identity as compared with neighbouring
parts of India?

The answers given to these questions will vary in
accordance with the concerns and interests of those through whose
eyes Goa is viewed in any particular period. In the seventeenth
century, as at other times, there were several distinct
perceptions or "images" of Goa, each held by an identifiable
interest group. First there was the Goa of the Portuguese crown
and administration which was conceived of as a distant royal
possession maintained for its strategic, economic and religious
importance to the metropolis, and for imperial prestige. Then
there was the Goa of the local elites – European merchants,
settlers, and officials in their private entrepreneurial
capacities, together with the Indians, mostly Brahmins and Banyas,
who collaborated with them in business and administration. To
these groups Goa was principally a funnel for commercial
enterprise. There was the Goa of the religious establishment,

especially of the great and powerful Roman Catholic regular orders, for whom Goa was an administrative and educational centre, and significant source of both recruits and income. Finally there was the more mundane Goa of the rural majority, which included both the traditional landowning class in the villages, and the great mass of landless labourers, fishermen and other underprivileged groups. What changes and continuities occurred in Goa during the seventeenth century, as they affected and were perceived by each of these four interest groups?

It has to be admitted that our knowledge of the Goan seventeenth century is still very incomplete, from whatever viewpoint Goa is seen. However, it is probably fair to say that, whereas the sixteenth century had been one of the key formative periods in Goa's evolution during which important features of her political, economic and cultural life took on more or less definitive shape, the seventeenth century was a period when many of these came under challenge, and much time and energy was expended in trying to protect and preserve them. Like contemporary Europe, Goa experienced a kind of seventeenth century crisis, which was at its most acute in the 1630s and 40s, and then again in the 1680s. Although Goa survived the seventeenth century crisis she emerged from it diminished, demographically, economically and politically.

It was the Goa of the Portuguese crown and administration that was most clearly challenged in the crisis of the seventeenth century, for the most obvious manifestations of the crisis were political and military. Portuguese control of Goa was threatened in the seventeenth century by two powerful external forces. During the first half of the century, and particularly acutely from about 1620, the most serious of these threats came from Portugal's European trade rivals, particularly the Dutch and to a lesser extent the English. As a result of the attacks of these European enemies Portugal lost, one by one, many of the most important and lucrative of her outlying possessions in Monsoon Asia. Ormuz, which was captured by the Persians with English naval backing in 1621, was the first to go, and was followed in the 1640s and 1650s by Malacca, and various strongpoints in Indonesia, Sri Lanka and the Malabar coast of southwest India, all of which fell before the Dutch assault. When a definitive Luso-Dutch treaty finally came into force in Asian waters in 1663, Portugal's presence in the region had been effectively reduced to little more than Goa, Damão, Bassein and Diu on the west coast of India, Macao off the south coast of China, part of Timor, and a few settlements on the coast of East Africa. Meanwhile, especially from the late 1630s through the 1650s, Goa itself was subjected to repeated blockades by Dutch naval forces.

Portuguese Goa was also under considerable pressure during much of the seventeenth century from several powerful Indian states located in its vicinity. These threats from the landward side emanated especially from the Sultanate of Bijapur in the early decades of the century and subsequently from a new and highly militant Hindu power, the Marathas, and from the great and still expanding Muslim-controlled empire of the Moghuls. Goa had been gripped by fear of an expected Bijapuri attack in the early 1630s, and experienced actual invasions from Bijapur in 1654 and 1659 which, in the event, were repelled successfully. In 1683 Goa was almost overwhelmed by the Marathas under Sambhaji, while the Moghuls, whose growing shadow had long been viewed with unease by the Portuguese viceroyalty, became the major cause of concern in the final years of the century.

The authorities of Goa were hopelessly ill-equipped with the necessary naval and military resources to combat these various enemies, and received little help from Portugal despite repeated appeals and warnings from officials on the spot. Even as early as the 1620s the Dutch, as a contemporary Portuguese report was forced to admit, had become 'absolute masters of the sea'.(1) Military weakness was matched by a deepening pessimism which touched even the viceroyalty itself, despite various examples of heroic and stubborn resistance by some Portuguese in defence of their imperial and commercial interests. To many contemporaries, both Portuguese and foreign, it seemed that the Lusitanian empire in Asia was doomed. Yet Portuguese Goa survived the century intact while other parts of the imperial structure crumbled around it. How can this rather unexpected success against the odds be explained?

Goa's survival in the face of her European enemies was partly a result of their failure to co-ordinate their attacks sufficiently either with each other or with potential Indian allies, and partly because the Portuguese, for all their military weakness, were too firmly entrenched to be shifted without a major and costly effort. Such an effort was hardly warranted from the point of view of hostile Eueropeans, for Goa had no significance as a producer, and little as an exporter of products from her own hinterland, while several other ports along the west coast of India could perform equally well her hitherto important role as an entrepot. Unless the Portuguese at Goa themselves behaved too provocatively the capital of the Estado da India could, therefore, be safely by-passed and ultimately ignored by a stronger naval power like the Dutch, whose primary objective was profits rather than dominion. The Dutch, despite their repeated blockades between 1638 and 1663, in practice made no serious attempt to seize and occupy Goa. Portuguese fears of a Spanish attack in the 1640s following Lisbon's revolt against the rule of Philip IV, proved equally unfounded. Nor did the English ever seriously threaten to seize Goa, although they were often at loggerheads with the Portuguese off western India, particularly until the truce signed between their viceroy and the president of the East India Company's factory at Surat in 1635.

The most serious challenge to Portuguese hegemony in Goa in the seventeenth century was undoubtedly that presented by the Marathas in the 1680s. At the time of Sambhaji's invasion, so desperate was the position believed to be by the viceroy, the Count of Alvor (1681-86), that he was reduced to the expedient of opening the tomb of St Francis Xavier, handing the dead saint his letters patent and baton of office, and begging him to take charge of the defences and perform the miracle which Alvor believed could alone save Portuguese Goa. The city would almost certainly have fallen on this occasion but for a sudden diversionary attack on the Marathas by the Moghuls, which forced Sambhaji hastily to withdraw his forces. Enmity among the Indian powers, their equivocal attitudes to the need and even desirability of expelling the Portuguese, who were sometimes seen as useful counters in the power game and sometimes as simply unimportant, contributed substantially to Goa's avoidance of conquest by land in the seventeenth century.

However, if Goa survived as part of the Portuguese maritime empire in 1700, she did not survive unscathed. Largely as a consequence of increasing defence costs together with declining revenues, Goa had ceased to be profitable to the crown from the early years of the century, if not before. It can be shown, for example, that crown revenue from the customs house at Goa fell sharply during roughly the years of Spanish Habsburg rule (1580-1640), and the quantity of pepper exported through Goa to Lisbon in the 1620s and 1630s under crown monopoly was less than half the sixteenth century average. The twin Portuguese strategies of trying to prey on regional trade through a forced licensing system, and imposing monopolies on certain key trade commodities, had to all intents and purposes failed by the early years of the century. The viceregal government was reduced to dire financial straits as a result of these developments, while the plight of the Goa câmara (municipal council) was probably even worse.

The impact of the seventeenth century crisis on the private sector of the Goan economy and the reactions of the key entrepreneurial groups are rather more complex. In the sixteenth century Goa had become one of the leading maritime entrepots on the western coast of India, but it is clear that conditions in the seventeenth century were much less favourable to this role. Most of the limited evidence we have, both qualitative and quantitative, in fact points to a sharp decline in Goa's maritime trade in the early decades of the new century, in relative and in absolute terms. On the other hand it would be premature to conclude on the basis of what is really known, that private business based on Goa was consistently depressed throughout the seventeenth century, or that it necessarily suffered to the same degree as the state. Such quantitative data as are available from this period are fragmentary in both time and scope, not particularly reliable and, except for a few individual commodities such as pepper, inadequate for even minimal serialization. Nearly all relate to government revenue and the crown trading monopolies rather than to the extensive network of individual and corporate interests which possessed far more flexibility and adaptibility than the official structure. These private business interests and those of the state were often at variance in Goa in the seventeenth century. M. N. Pearson has remarked on the lack of patriotism among the casados (married settlers) of Portuguese India, who usually put their private affairs before the state – and the same could be said of virtually all identifiable groups who played a role in Goan trade, including not only European and Hindu businessmen, but less obviously the great religious corporations, and even, and often most spectacularly, key crown officials not excluding the viceroys themselves, in their private capacities.(2)

There were, broadly speaking, two contrasting images of the state of private business enterprise in Goa, the one negative and the other positive, especially for the first half of the seventeenth century. On the negative side there was a continuing chorus of complaints from the camara, and in the correspondence of the period generally, stressing and bewailing the alleged depressed state of trade and the poverty of the times. Undoubtedly these complaints had some justification, for certain kinds of economic activity became appreciably more difficult and less profitable in the early seventeenth century, seriously damaging the interests of those traditionally involved in them. Long-distance ocean trading was particularly vulnerable, such as the immensely profitable trade with China and Japan through Macao. This was severely disrupted by the Dutch in the early decades of the century and the link with Japan was then completely severed by the Japanese after 1639. But other avenues for profit still remained open. It was possible for Goa-based entrepreneurs to concentrate more on India itself and on the Indian coastal trades. Fortunes could be made in Goa through trading in commodity foodstuffs, in diamonds and, increasingly in the late seventeenth century, in opium. Goa-based private entrepreneurs were not, of course, confined to activity in Portuguese-controlled areas, but traded freely across political boundaries with anyone and everyone, wherever business could be driven. In the more settled conditions of the later seventeenth century a particularly lucrative trade was also carried on through Portuguese possessions and points of contact in East Africa.

Dazzling successes were still sometimes achieved by private enterprise in Goa during this period, a fact strikingly illustrated by the huge fortunes repeatedly made by certain high functionaries of the Portuguese administration. The viceroy Count of Linhares (1629-35), who was aptly called by a contemporary 'the most skillful merchant and Chetty that India ever had' allegedly made almost half a million cruzados out of grain profiteering alone during the great famine of 1630-1.(3) He returned home

laden with riches in 1636, and presented King Philip IV, Queen
Isabella and the Crown Prince Baltasar Carlos with gifts of
diamonds worth in all about 100,000 ducats. Viceroy Dom Felipe
Mascarenhas (1645-51) accumulated a personal collection of superb
diamonds in India, and diamonds also underlay the Indian fortune
of Viceroy Dom Lourenco de Almeida acquired in 1697-1704. But
perhaps the greatest of all viceregal fortunes of the seventeenth
century was that acquired by the Viceroy Count of Lavradio who set
out on his return voyage to Lisbon in 1677 taking with him a
personal fortune alleged to amount to two million cruzados, made
mostly from the East African trade. Unfortunately for Lavradio
his ship was lost before it reached home and he himself died. But
he had previously taken the precaution of investing some four to
five million cruzados in various European banks. By contrast, in
1638 the Goa government found itself in the embarrassing situation
of being unable to provide a diamond-studded cross as a present
for the Sultan of Atjeh, because the treaury lacked the necessary
cash to pay for it, and no jeweller would provide the item on
credit.

The great viceregal fortunes of the seventeenth century
were made in collaboration with both expatriate European and local
Indian businessmen. A significant number of European merchants of
substance, both Portuguese and foreign, flourished in Goa,
especially during the first four decades of the seventeenth
century. Among them were men like the Portuguese Manuel de Moraes
Supico who died in 1630 after many years successful business in
Monsoon Asia and whose rich tomb in Goa cathedral attests to his
success, and the Flemish brothers Jacques and Joseph de Couttre
who remained active in Goan trade for three decades between 1592
and 1623, making large sums from buying and selling Indian
diamonds. A recent seminal study by James Boyajian on the
activities of Portuguese bankers at the court of Philip IV
documents the extraordinarily widespread international business
networks maintained by the Portuguese-Jewish banking firms in the
first half of the seventeenth century, many of whom placed a
representative, often a family member, in Goa during these
years.(4) Similar arrangements were made by various foreign
European trading interests which operated out of Goa early in the
century, mostly Italians, Flemings or South Germans. Early
seventeenth century Goa was therefore an international trading
centre with considerable worldwide ramifications. But none of the
various European interests which prospered in Goa could have done
so without the co-operation and help of Indian, particularly
Hindu, entrepreneurs who continued to dominate the administration
of the local economy and to provide indispensable inputs of
capital and local knowledge essential to both the Portuguese
colonial government and expatriate private trade. Viceroy
Linhares in the early 1630s could not have made his sizeable
fortune without the help of his Indian friend and collaborator,
the Banya Rama Keni. The resilience of the Hindu entrepreneur in

Goa is striking and some families, like the Kenis and the Ranes, appear to have retained their prominence for centuries.

While there is no doubt therefore that private fortunes, sometimes of a spectacular kind, were made in Goa in the seventeenth century, and that the European nabob was a Portuguese phenomenon before he became an English one, the present state of knowledge does not permit the historian to determine very precisely how extensive and how well-sustained as the century progressed overall business prosperity was. It is, however, clear that there were serious obstacles to be overcome by the Goa-based entrepreneur, of whatever origin, during the first half of the seventeenth century, and that as time proceeded there was less and less incentive for him to remain centred in Goa. As a hub of international trade Goa clearly declined in comparative importance during the course of the century. At the same time she suffered a steady and apparently irreversible fall in population, which was not the least manifestation of her seventeenth century crisis. The loss of population appears to have begun sometime in the 1570s, and was very marked by the 1630s when one well-informed contemporary claimed many suburbs had become virtually deserted, and the city had shrunk to about a third of its former numbers. Goa's population was hard hit by the great famine of 1631-2, and the city acquired such a reputation for unhealthiness that, particularly from the time of Viceroy Alvor in the 1680s, the Portuguese began seriously to consider moving the capital to another site. This was eventually done in the following century when the administrative apparatus was shifted several miles down river to Panjim. Meanwhile, the Goan business community steadily contracted in size as the city population in general fell, and rival entrepots grew stronger.

Under these circumstances there was an increasing tendency for businessmen to conduct operations outside Goa itself, and outside of the official Portuguese networks. During his almost 32 years as a Goa-based merchant Jacques de Couttre spent far more time travelling and trading in various parts of India and the Middle East, such as the diamond mines of Golconda, the courts at Agra and Bijapur, and the Syrian city of Aleppo, than he did in Goa itself. The revival of interest in the overland routes to Europe from Goa via Ormuz until its fall to the Persians, and then via Muscat, as an alternative to the Cape route, which had been somewhat evident in the early decades of the century, petered out as far the Portuguese were concerned from the early 1640s. By the 1640s Goa and the Portuguese possessions in Asia generally were no longer indispensable to non-Portuguese Europeans trading the region, as the northern European chartered companies provided reliable alternative means of seaborne transport to Europe and established their own network of factories and trade contacts. Surat became the principal port of export for western India in the early decades of the century, and soon afterwards Madras replaced Goa as the chief outlet for Indian diamonds. While it is true that other lines such as opium, and the gold, ivory, hardwoods and slaves of East Africa still made private fortunes possible for Goa-based entrepreneurs in the later seventeenth century, there seems little doubt that Goa per se, and in comparison with its regional rivals, had suffered considerable diminution by this period.

Compared with the gloomy image of Goa as a crown possession in the seventeenth century and the more complex and equivocal Goa of private enterprise, Goa as seen through religious eyes, and particularly those of the great Roman Catholic missionary orders, appeared in a much more optimistic light. Charles Boxer has claimed that a spirit of virtual triumphalism pervaded the missionary correspondence of the seventeenth century.(5) Despite the brutal persecutions which by 1640 had virtually wiped out the christian communities of Japan, so heroically built up by the Jesuits in the preceding century, missionary leaders were more often than not in a buoyant and expansive mood, especially finding encouragement in the promising progress of their missions in Vietnam and South China. The headquarters of all the Portuguese missionary orders in Asia were located in Goa, and their confidence and solidity is demonstrated by the extraordinary ecclesiastical architecture of the era.

The florescent period of Goan religious architecture was the late sixteenth and early seventeenth centuries. The two most important Catholic buildings in Goa - the Se' Cathedral (begun 1562, but still undergoing final construction and embellishment in the 1630s) and the huge Augustinian convent-church of Our Lady of Grace (built between 1597 and 1602) - date from these years. Both buildings acted as models for many fine Mannerist churches constructed in Goa and the Goan territories during the course of the seventeenth century, such as the parish churches of Cortalim and Rachol. Often with lavishly decorated interiors displaying a mixture of Portuguese and Indian motifs, including magnificent cobra-headed canopies and intricate patterns of roses of Iran and angels in saris, many of these edifices have retained their splendour to this day. In the seventeenth century a special prominence and prestige had already been accorded the great Jesuit basilica of the Bom Jesus (built between 1594 and 1605) which contained the magnificent tomb of St Francis Xavier, patron saint of the East, who was canonised in 1622 and whose sanctified body reposed in an extraordinary tomb executed in 1636-7 by Goan craftsmen, Italianate in design, but covered in oriental filigree like an Indian marble casket.

If the seventeenth century came closer to being a gilded age for the Catholic religious in Goa than it did for any other interest group (except perhaps for viceroys and other high functionaries in their private entrepreneurial capacities) the alleged opulence of the orders aroused a great deal of resentment on the part of non-members. The extent of this opulence and material prosperity still remains a matter for debate. The economic activities of the various orders based at Goa, particularly the Jesuits, have attracted considerable interest in recent years, especially in the work, completed or still in progress, of Charles Boxer, Teotinio de Souza and Dauril Alden. Boxer has depicted the Jesuits as a kind of prototype of the modern multinational corporation, with a more varied and extensive network of business operations in the seventeenth century than either the Dutch or the English East India Companies.(6) This claim will have to await the completetion of Alden's massive study of the economic activities of the Jesuits in the Portuguese world before it can be fully borne out or not. But it does appear that the Jesuits were able to adjust relatively well to changing conditions by careful management, and by concentrating more of their commercial activities outside the formal boundaries of Portuguese territory.

The power of the religious orders in Goa in the first half of the seventeenth century was undoubtedly considerable, and it has even been claimed that the Jesuits were more influential than the viceroys. Viceroy Linhares accused them in 1631 of wanting to take over the royal jurisdiction, and most of his seventeenth century predecessors and successors shared his suspicions and dislike of alleged Jesuit interference in state affairs. In Goa early in the century, when their influence was at its peak, the Jesuits were believed to dispose of a massive investment not only in trade but in land and other forms of real estate. The Jesuits together with the other regulars were seen to be too numerous, their presence too pervasive, and their share of dwindling resources to maintain their level of operations too great to go unchallenged. Complaints were particularly loud against the Jesuit and Franciscan accumulation of landed property, and the orders were eventually obliged to relinquish some of their holdings after a series of investigations towards the end of the first half of the century.

By the beginning of the seventeenth century the Goan christian community had become reasonably settled and constituted a majority of the population, but a practising Hindu minority still survived in Portuguese territory. Despite legal restrictions, Hinduism was, on the whole, more tolerated in Goa in the seventeenth century than it had been in the sixteenth, and even the Inquisition tended to be pragmatic in its handling of crypto-Hindus. In the early 1690s almost 30,000 Hindus were said to be living in Goa, many of them in what amounted to Hindu ghettos in the city.(7) Any serious attempt by the viceroyalty to clamp down on these communities would have brought probably unsurmountable problems to the Portuguese administration given the key role played by Hindus in the Goan economy, and it was therefore not surprising that a request from an unusually zealous Inquisition board in 1691 to expel the Hindus received a non-committal answer.

Until relatively recently modern historians have shown
little interest in the effect of the seventeenth century crisis on
rural Goa, despite the quite substantial body of relevant
information which lay buried in the older and voluminous works of
J. H. Cunha Rivara and Felipe Nery Xavier.(8)   T. R. de Souza's
valuable monograph, Medieval Goa, is an important step towards
rectifying this.   The fundamental institution of rural life in
seventeenth century Goa was the village community (communidade),
whose origins long pre-dated the Portuguese conquest.   The village
lands were owned and controlled in common by the community members
who were known as ganvkars.   These men, an elite minority of the
rural inhabitants who acquired their rights by inheritance from
father to son, were mostly high-caste Brahmins and Kshatriyas.
They formed a closed and exclusive group from which the majority
of the rural populace, the landless labourers made up of low-caste
Shudras, Gaudas and Kunbis, was excluded.   How did these rural
groups fare in the Goan seventeenth century ?

The rural policy of the Portuguese government was to
maintain the status quo - to preserve the communidades and the
privileges of the ganvkars, and to interfere as little as possible
in their affairs.   In return, the communidades paid land tax to
the state.   Except to receive taxes, to impose occasional manpower
levies and to promote and protect Roman Catholicism, the
viceroyalty showed only minimal interest in life at the village
level.   There is no evidence of any official interest in
agricultural productivity per se before the eighteenth century,
except perhaps by Viceroy António da Camara Coutinho (1698-1701)
at the very end of the period, who came to Goa with an excellent
reputation for crop experimentation and development gained in
Brazil.

Despite the conservatism of the viceregal administration,
it is apparent that the entrenched position of the communidades in
rural life came under increasing pressure from outside forces
during the first half of the seventeenth century.   Already in the
previous century much land in the vicinity of the city had been
reallocated to individual Portuguese, and when the missionary
campaign got under way and Hindu temples were systematically
eradicated, the village lands formerly assigned to their keep were
given to the Catholic orders.   In the early decades of the
seventeenth century the process of alienation intensified, with
considerable competition to acquire land between the Catholic
religious, Portuguese settlers, and non-ganvkar Hindu outsiders.
Acquiring land was seen partly as an alternative to investing in
maritime trade which was becoming more risky as the state's
ability to protect shipping weakened.   The state itself, despite
its support in principle for the communidades, contributed to the
process of alienation by confiscating the lands of various
villages as a form of collective punishment for alleged rebellion,
and granting them to individuals who, in turn, sometimes passed
them on to the religious.

In the first half of the century there were frequent complaints from both individual communidades and the general assemblies of Salcete and Bardez, the two major rural districts of Goa, against encroachments on village landownership and abuse of the privileges of ganvkars. Repeated instructions and policy pronouncements from the crown, reinforced by decrees and judicial decisions from the Goan government, went some way towards containing the trend to alienation but the forces involved were too strong to be easily halted. In a long petition addressed to John IV in 1642 the general assembly of Salcete asked for a secret inquiry by the Inquisition, claiming this was the only body strong enough to stand up to the Jesuits. Individual Portuguese residents, the Goa câmara and occasionally viceroys themselves, also complained about the engrossing of land by the orders. Eventually, despite various delays and attempted evasions, detailed inventories of the land and property holdings of the various religious orders were drawn up. The Jesuits were dispossessed of their landholdings in Salcete in 1646, but apparently still continued to dominate its villages long thereafter. A declaration in 1649 that land was not owned outright by the communidades but held on lease from the crown, and was therefore inalienable, though legally dubious, was a reasonably effective measure against further erosion of the system. In the final analysis it would seem that the Goan communidades survived the seventeenth century quite well, and that they were able to confine to manageable proportions outside infiltration, which at one stage threatened to develop into a serious challenge to traditional ganvkar hegemony.

For the less privileged groups in Goa's rural population, mostly made up of landless labourers and their families, life was always precarious, and the seventeenth century crisis probably made little practical difference. Of course, those living near the margins of subsistence were particularly vulnerable to the ravages of invading armies from Bijapur in the 1650s, and from the Marathas in the 1680s, as also from the devastating famine and pestilence of 1630–31. Goa was a permanent grain-deficit area in the seventeenth century, heavily dependent on rice imported by sea, though some rural districts were usually self-sufficient for at least part of the year. The result was considerable fluctuations in the availability of basic foodstuffs and instability of prices, which exacerbated the insecurity of both rural and urban poor. Under these circumstances, the failure of the vicerergal government to do anything significant to improve agriculture for virtually 250 years until the belated reforms instigated by the Marquis de Pombal in the 1770s, seems rather surprising. Goa obtained her rice imports primarily by shipping them from the supply ports of Gujerat to the north and Kanara to the south, while some grain was also brought overland from the interior via Bjapur. But for much of the seventeenth century maritime communications were disrupted by the Dutch and by local corsairs, while there were periodic closures of the land borders.

It would therefore seem that there was good reason to try to maximise local production in the seventeenth century and strictly to control exports. Viceroy Linhares did once express the view that Goa would be better off if it could take possession of all of the surrounding territory up to the foothills of the Ghats, but he seems to have had defence more in mind than agricultural capacity. In the late seventeenth century controls were so lax and profiteering so rife that foodstuffs were apparently flowing out to the neighbouring state of Bijapur on a large scale, rather then the reverse.

Despite their reputation as over-mighty landholders which roused such resentment in some quarters, the Jesuits were in certain respects a positive influence on rural Goa. They were more efficient farmers and managers than most other landholders, operated on a bigger scale, were more sympathetic to experimentation and improvement, and tended to achieve higher yields. The Jesuits also sought to protect the village communities from a variety of threats - from better-off and more acquisitive individual villagers, from encroaching outsiders, and sometimes also from the state. They advanced seed to farmers who lacked it, sought to have oppressive officials removed or brought to justice, and tried to mitigate the manpower demands of the Portuguese administration, especially on their own villages. Such activities inevitably brought the Jesuits into the political arena, and contributed materially to their constant bickering with the viceregal authorities, so characteristic especially of the first two decades of the century.

The crisis of the seventeenth century forced the viceregal government to make more and increasingly burdensome demands on its own rural hinterland in an effort to make up for the resources it so patently lacked and so desperately needed. These demands were partly economic and partly military. In 1614 a form of militia service was introduced for the male population of Salcete. They were organised into companies, given some training and required to attend a muster twice yearly. In 1631 the viceroy ordered the Salcete and Bardez communidades to provide 900 men between them for service in Sri Lanka. The Bardez quota was raised without too much protest but considerable resistance, in part inspired by the Jesuits, was encountered in Salcete, and was only overcome with much trouble. The next viceroy forced Salcete to provide contingents for garrison duty in various places including the important fortress of Mormugão, to be maintained at the expense of the villages. Exemptions from military service were later promised in return for a cash subsidy from the Salcete assembly; but once this had been paid recruits were soon being demanded once again. Other extraordinary tax levies were extracted from time to time, such as the sum of 6000 ashrafi collected by Viceroy Linhares to build a new fort, but more important was a whole series of new regular charges, including an increase in the customs rate, taxes on tobacco and arrack, and above all a tax on foodstuffs known as <u>collecta</u>. There is therefore some evidence that in the seventeenth century imperial administration was weighing more heavily on the Goans, including those in the villages, despite the Portuguese preference for minimal change.

What did Goans think about the continuance of Portuguese rule in their territory during the seventeenth century, and what was the extent and significance of internal opposition to it? Is it possible to discern in this period the antecedents of Goan nationalism, and of the liberation movement that culminated in the expulsion of the Portuguese in 1961? Setting aside the question of whether the inhabitants of the region self-consciously considered themselves "Indians" or even "Goans" in the seventeenth century, there is in fact very little evidence to suggest the existence of such antecedents. What internal opposition there was to Portuguese rule appears to have been the product of individual or at most sectional grievances, and failed to galvanise popular support to any significant degree. The acquiescence and docility displayed by the vast majority of Goans to Portuguese rule must have been the despair of those few who were dedicated to its overthrow. The lusophobe Goan cleric Mattheus de Castro plotted against the Portuguese incessantly with whomever he could in the middle years of the century, including such disparate and mutually hostile forces as the Dutch, the Spaniards, the Bijapuris and Moghuls. In 1644, living just over the Goa border in Bicholim, he informed Philip IV of Spain that the Spaniards, with the aid of Bijapur, could easily take Goa and then the whole Estado da India with just three or four galleons. Clearly this was wishful thinking, as was his wildly optimistic assurance to the Bijapuris that if they invaded Bardez and Salcete they would be supported by a mass uprising against Portuguese rule, a claim proved quite inaccurate when put to the test in 1654. Apart from a few acts of sabotage, which were ruthlessly punished, the populace of Goa remained quiescent during the crisis years of the seventeenth century, even if there was no particularly enthusiastic endorsement of Portuguese rule.

Most Goans, like most Indians in the sub-continent generally, appear to have viewed political authority philosophically and passively. It was a fact of life which had to be put up with, but people avoided unnecessary involvement with it rather than actively opposing or embracing it. If the behaviour of the state became intolerable to the average Goan, it was usually easier to flee across the nearby border than to rebel. Many people both from the city and rural Goa did in fact emigrate in the seventeenth century, sometimes permanently but probably more often temporarily. They included Christians as well as Hindus. In 1693 an Inquisitorial visitation discovered that numerous Goan Christians from Salcete were living in neighbouring India for periods of ten, fifteen or even twenty years, intermarrying with local Hindus and often failing to have their children baptized.(9) The text implies, however, that many of the emigrants ultimately returned. It seems that Goans of the seventeenth century were as inclined as those of the twentieth to leave home to seek a better livelihood, while at the same time consciously maintaining their roots and sentimental attachments in their native villages. Village loyalty was, in all probability, a more potent force than Goan nationalism in the "century of crisis".

Notes

1. Cited in A.Disney, Twilight of the Pepper Empire (Cambridge Mass., 1978) p.65.

2. M.N.Pearson, Coastal Western India (New Delhi, 1981) p.60.

3. Biblioteca Nacional, Lisbon, Colleccão Pombalina, Codex 490, f. 180v.

4. James Boyajian, Portuguese Bankers at the Court of Spain, 1626-1650 (New Brunswick, 1983).

5. C.R.Boxer, Portuguese India in the Mid-Seventeenth Century (Delhi, 1980) p.14.

6. Ibid pp.49-50.

7. Document published in T.R.de Souza, Medieval Goa (Delhi, 1979) appendix A-12.

8. J.H. da Cunha Rivara, Ensaio historico da Lingua Concani (Nova Goa, 1858); F.N. Xavier, Leis Peculiares das Comunidades Agricolas das Ilhas Salcete e Bardez, 2 vols (Nova Goa, 1852-55), and Bosequejo historico das comunidades, 4 parts (Nova Goa, 1852).

9. Souza, Medieval Goa, appendix A-12.

BIBLIOGRAPHICAL NOTES

General and Introductory

All English readers approaching the study of the first Portuguese empire must rely on certain basic introductory works. Of these certainly the most important is C.R.Boxer, The Portuguese Seaborne Empire (London, 1969). This book examines various topics but does not seek to give a chronological account of developments. Covering the fifteenth and sixteenth centuries in some detail, and with a broadly chronological framework, is B.Diffie and G.Winius, Foundations of the Portuguese Empire 1415-1580 (Oxford, 1977). Holden Furber, Rival Empires of Trade in the Orient 1600-1800 (Minneapolis, 1976) is the second volume in the same series. G.V.Scammell, The World Encompassed (London, 1981) is a recent introduction to all the European commercial empires. Without question the best available general history of Portugal available in English is A.H.de Oliveira Marques, A History of Portugal, 2 vols, (New York, 1972).

Prince Henry and the Origins of Portuguese Expansion

The older English "classics" on the Portuguese discoveries are still found on most library shelves. Among those recently reissued are H.Major, The Life of Prince Henry the Navigator (London, 1868, reissued 1967), C.R.Beazley, Prince Henry the Navigator (New York, 1895, reissued 1968) and Edgar Prestage, The Portuguese Pioneers (London, 1933, reissued 1966). None of the works of the leading Portuguese historians has been translated into English which makes Bailley Diffie's contribution to Foundations of the Portuguese Empire all the more important as it is based on an exhaustive study of the Portuguese literature and has a fine bibliography. The best exploration of the broader economic background to the discoveries is Pierre Chaunu, European Expansion in the Later Middle Ages, trans. K.Bertram, (Oxford, 1979). A few important monographs have appeared in English. Bailley Diffie's, Prelude to Empire (Lincoln, Nebraska, 1960) explores the economic and maritime expansion of Portugal prior to the fifteenth century. T.Bentley Duncan, The Atlantic Islands (Chicago, 1972) is a good introduction to the history of Madeira, the Azores and Cape Verde Islands. A.C.de M.C.Saunders, A Social History of Black Slaves and Freedmen in Portugal 1441-1555 (Cambridge, 1982) is an important breakthrough into the history of Portugal itself. C.Nowell, 'Prince Henry the Navigator and his Brother Dom Pedro', Hispanic America Historical Review, 1948, pp.62-67 is still useful as an introduction to the debate about the role of the two princes. Three collections of source material have been available for some time in editions of the Hakluyt Society: C.R.Beazley and E.Prestage eds., The Discovery and Conquest of Guinea, 2 vols, 1896-9; G.R.Crone ed. The Voyages of Cadamosto, 1937; and J.W.Blake, Europeans in West Africa, 2 vols, 1942.

The Estado da India in Southeast Asia

The Most recent work that attempts to give a general definition of the Estado da India as well as a detailed description of its institutions is A.T.de Matos, O Estado da India nos anos de 1581-1588: estrutura administrativa e economica (Ponta Delgada, 1982). To gain a general idea of the situation during the brief period of Portuguese dominance in Indonesian waters see J.C. van Leur, Indonesian Trade and Society (The Hague and Bandung, 1955) and M.A.P.Meilink-Roelofsz, Asian Trade and European Influence in the Indonesian Archipelago between 1500 and about 1630 (The Hague, 1962). Works by C.R.Boxer bearing on the Portuguese in the East include: Portuguese India in the mid-Seventeenth Century (Oxford, 1980); Fidalgos in the Far East (Oxford, 1968), especially the chapter entitled 'Turbulent Timor'; Portuguese Society in the Tropics: the Municipal Councils of Goa, Macao, Bahia and Luanda 1510-1600 (Wisconsin, 1965); The Great Ship from Amacon: annals of Macao and the Old Japan Trade 1555-1640 (Lisbon, 1963). No student of Timor can afford to ignore A.T.de Matos, Timor Portuguese 1515-1769 (Lisbon, 1974) and for the Moluccas H.Jacobs SJ ed., Treatise on the Moluccas, a translation of Antonio Galvão's work of c.1544. Finally Georg Schurhammer's monumental biography Francis Xavier, his life and his times, 4 vols, (Rome, 1974-82) deserves a special mention as it is much more than just a life of the "apostle of the Indies" but an enormous panoramic survey of all those parts of Asia where the Jesuit missions worked.

Trade in the Indian Ocean and the Portuguese System of Cartazes

The economic history of the Portuguese empire in the East has been dealt with in magisterial fashion by Vitorino Magalhães Godinho. None of his works are available in English but the one most accessible for English readers is L'Economie de l'Empire Portugais (Paris, 1969). The Cambridge Economic History of India, vol 1, edited by T.Raychaudhuri and I.Habib, (Cambridge, 1982) is also fundamental background reading. M.N.Pearson, Merchants and Rulers in Gujerat (Berkeley, 1976) gives an excellent introduction to Portuguese commercial activities in western India and to the cartaz system and these are discussed further in K.S.Mathew, Portuguese Trade with India in the Sixteenth Century (New Delhi, 1983). Some of the basic Portuguese material is available in English translation in the publications of the Hakluyt Society. Of greatest importance are, Tomé Pires, Suma Oriental, Armando Cortesão ed., 1944 and M.L.Dames ed., The Book of Duarte Barbosa, 2 vols, 1918-21. For the decline of the commercial empire in the seventeenth century see A.R.Disney, Twilight of the Pepper Empire: Portuguese Trade in Southwest India in the early seventeenth century (Cambridge Mass., 1978) and N.Steensgaard, The Asiatic Trade Revolution of the Seventeenth Century (Chicago, 1975).

Goa in the Seventeenth Century

The best recent survey is C.R.Boxer, Portuguese India in the Mid-Seventeenth Century which includes many penetrating insights from the doyen of Portuguese overseas history and numerous useful footnote references. There is no adequate study of the Portuguese administrastion in Goa in the seventeenth century, but for social and economic history T.R.de Souza, Medieval Goa: a Socio-Economic History (Delhi, 1979) is a pioneering work of seminal importance, with much of value for this period. Other relevant works in English that have been published in the last ten years or so, each dealing with a specialist topic or topics include, in order of publication, A.R.Disney, Twilight of the Pepper Empire; M.N.Pearson, Coastal Western India (Delhi, 1981); P.S.Pissurlencar, The Portuguese and the Marathas, P.R.Kakodkar trans., (Delhi, 1975). The best book on art and architecture is Carlos de Azevedo, A Arte de Goa, Damão e Diu (Lisbon, 1970), unfortunately not available in English. Various papers presented to two international seminars on Indo-Portuguese History held in Goa in 1978 and 1983 respectively were published as Indo-Portuguese History - Sources and Problems, John Correia-Afonso ed., (Bombay, 1981) and Indo-Portuguese History: Old Issues, New Questions, T.R.de Souza ed., (Delhi, 1985). Many more works in English, Portuguese and other languages are listed in the bibliographies and footnotes of these publications and in Henry Scholberg, Bibliography of Goa and the Portuguese in India (Delhi, 1982).

BIOGRAPHICAL NOTES

A.R.Disney   Senior Lecturer in the History Department at La Trobe University in Melbourne, Australia. He is currently working on a biography of Dom Miguel de Noronha, fourth Count of Linhares, who was viceroy at Goa between 1629 and 1635. He recently spent eight months as a member of the Institute of Advanced Study at Princeton and is author of Twilight of the Pepper Empire.

K.S.Mathew   Professor of History at Maharajah Sayajirao University, Baroda, India. He is the author of Portuguese Trade with India in the Sixteenth Century and articles on the economic history of India in the sixteenth century.

M.D.D.Newitt   Senior Lecturer in History at Exeter University and formerly lecturer in the University College of Rhodesia. He is the author of Portuguese Settlement on the Zambesi, Portugal In Africa, and The Comoro Islands.

J.Villiers   Director of the British Institute in South-East Asia, Bangkok, Thailand. He is author of articles on the Portuguese in eastern Indonesia and is editor of the South-East Asian Studies Newsletter.

EXETER STUDIES IN HISTORY

EXETER STUDIES IN HISTORY is a paperback series produced by the Department of History and Archaeology at the University of Exeter. Each issue is devoted to the examination of a major historical theme or problem. The series aims primarily at a readership among undergraduates and sixth formers. Other titles in the series:

ESH 1 The Military Revolution and the State, 1500-1800, edited by Michael Duffy (1980)

ESH 2 Government, Party and People in Nazi Germany, edited by Jeremy Noakes (1980)

ESH 3 'Into Another Mould': Aspects of the Interregnum, edited by Ivan Roots (1981)

ESH 4 Problems and Case Studies in Archaeological Dating, edited by Bryony Orme (1982)

ESH 5 Britain and Revolutionary France: Conflict, Subversion and Propaganda, edited by Colin Jones (1983)

ESH 6 Nazism 1919-1945. Volume 1. The Rise to Power, 1919-1934, edited by Jeremy Noakes and Geoffrey Pridham (1983)

ESH 7 Roman Political Life 90BC-AD69, edited by Peter Wiseman (1985)

ESH 8 Nazism 1919-1945. Volume 2. State, Economy and Society, 1933-1939, edited by Jeremy Noakes and Geoffrey Pridham (1984)

ESH 9 Africa, America and Central Asia: Formal and Informal Empire in the Nineteenth Century, edited by Peter Morris (1984)

ESH 10 'Raleigh in Exeter 1985': Privateering and Colonization in the Reign of Elizabeth I, edited by Joyce Youings (1985)

For information on these and other titles in history and archaeology produced by the University of Exeter, please write to the Publications Office, Reed Hall, University of Exeter, Exeter EX4 4QJ.